Cambridge Elements ≡

Elements in Perception
edited by
James T. Enns
The University of British Columbia

Special Editor for Attention
Marvin Chun
Yale College

CROSSMODAL ATTENTION APPLIED

Lessons for Driving

Charles Spence
University of Oxford

Salvador Soto-Faraco
ICREA and Universitat Pompeu Fabra

CAMBRIDGE
UNIVERSITY PRESS

CAMBRIDGE
UNIVERSITY PRESS

University Printing House, Cambridge CB2 8BS, United Kingdom

One Liberty Plaza, 20th Floor, New York, NY 10006, USA

477 Williamstown Road, Port Melbourne, VIC 3207, Australia

314–321, 3rd Floor, Plot 3, Splendor Forum, Jasola District Centre, New Delhi – 110025, India

79 Anson Road, #06–04/06, Singapore 079906

Cambridge University Press is part of the University of Cambridge.

It furthers the University's mission by disseminating knowledge in the pursuit of education, learning, and research at the highest international levels of excellence.

www.cambridge.org
Information on this title: www.cambridge.org/9781108826501
DOI: 10.1017/9781108919951

First published 2020

A catalogue record for this publication is available from the British Library.

ISBN 978-1-108-82650-1 Paperback
ISSN 2515-0502 (online)
ISSN 2515-0499 (print)

Cambridge University Press has no responsibility for the persistence or accuracy of URLs for external or third-party internet websites referred to in this publication and does not guarantee that any content on such websites is, or will remain, accurate or appropriate.

Crossmodal Attention Applied

Lessons for Driving

Elements in Perception

DOI: 10.1017/ 9781108919951
First published online: August 2020

Charles Spence
University of Oxford

Salvador Soto-Faraco
ICREA and Universitat Pompeu Fabra

Author for correspondence: Charles Spence, charles.spence@psy.ox.ac.uk

Abstract: Cognitive neuroscientists have started to uncover the neural substrates, systems, and mechanisms enabling us to prioritize the processing of certain sensory information over other, currently less-relevant, inputs. However, there is still a large gap between the knowledge generated in the laboratory and its application to real-life problems of attention as when, for example, interface operators are multitasking. In this Element, laboratory studies on crossmodal attention (both behavioural/psychophysical and cognitive neuroscience) are situated within the applied context of driving. We contrast the often idiosyncratic conditions favoured by much of the laboratory research, typically using a few popular paradigms involving simplified experimental conditions, with the noisy, multisensory, real-world environments filled with complex, intrinsically meaningful stimuli. By drawing attention to the differences between basic and applied studies in the context of driving, we highlight a number of important issues and neglected areas of research as far as the study of crossmodal attention is concerned.

Keywords: crossmodal attention, multisensory integration, spatial, applied, cognitive neuroscience, driving

ISBNs: 9781108826501 (PB), 9781108919951 (OC)
ISSNs: 2515-0502 (online), ISSN 2515-0499 (print)

Contents

1 Introduction

Selective attention has been a focus of research interest among those working on the scientific study of human behaviour from its very beginnings (e.g., Geissler, 1909; Hylan, 1903; James, 1890; Ribot, 1898; Titchener, 1908; Woodrow, 1914). This cognitive function (or, as is probably more likely, set of functions) ensures, most of the time, that an observer's limited-capacity processing resources are allocated efficiently (see Lennie, 2003), as a function of external as well as endogenous factors (Chun, Golomb, & Turk-Browne, 2011). Over the last century or so, researchers interested in attention have increasingly widened the scope of their investigations out from a seemingly-narrow consideration of attention operating solely within a single sensory modality (i.e., focusing on audition, vision, and, more recently, touch) (Carrasco, 2011; Driver, 2001; Mondor & Zatorre, 1995; Scharf, 1998; Spence & Driver, 1994) to a broader consideration of how selection occurs in the more realistic, and often cluttered, multisensory environments of daily life (e.g., Spence & Driver, 2004; see also Pashler, Johnston, & Ruthruff, 2001).

At the same time, however, there has also been a rapid growth of interest from applied psychologists and human factors researchers wanting to use the findings and insights from the laboratory studies of crossmodal attention in order to try to help design more effective multisensory interfaces and warning signals for those working in a variety of real-world situations. These include everything from driving to flying, and from the operating theatre to the trading floor (e.g., see Baldwin et al., 2012; Deatherage, 1972; Ferris & Sarter, 2008, 2011; Ho & Spence, 2008; Ngo, Pierce, & Spence, 2012; Sarter, 2002, 2006, for selected research on these themes). However, the focus of this Element will primarily be on driving, given that is where the majority of the applied crossmodal attention research has been pub-lished. In particular, this Element will focus on key insights that have emerged from the laboratory study of crossmodal attention, which we then attempt to fit into the context of the constraints and demands faced by drivers (e.g., when attempting to multitask at the wheel) (Strayer & Drews, 2007).

Importantly, and as highlighted by a number of authors who have been advocating for cognitive neuroscience to have greater concern for matters of ecological validity, this attempt to generalize laboratory findings may help to bring about unexpected outcomes. Indeed, the hope is that this effort will reveal novel research questions that have not heretofore been addressed by those working solely in the laboratory setting (e.g., see de Gelder &

Bertelson, 2003; Hasson, Mallach, & Heeger, 2010; Maguire, 2012; Peelen & Kastner, 2014; Soto-Faraco et al., 2019; Wolfe, Horowitz, & Kenner, 2005). In this Element, each section starts by summarizing what is currently known on the basis of the extensive body of laboratory research that has been published, before turning the focus to a number of areas in crossmodal attention research that, despite being relevant to real-word settings, have simply not been studied (or else have seemingly been neglected) in the laboratory. Along the way, we draw attention to evident gaps between commonly used laboratory protocols and the actual processing demands the driver is confronted with under more realistic conditions (see Spence & Ho, 2015a, 2015b, for reviews).

To set the scene, and illustrate why it is not always a simple matter to extend from the laboratory to the real world, let us start by briefly describing what happened when Lee and Spence (2015) attempted to adapt Spence and Driver's (1997a) basic laboratory-based crossmodal attention paradigm to the context of driving. Spence and Driver demonstrated that auditory cues suddenly appearing at one side of a person automatically summon the person's visual attention to the side of space on which the cue is presented, even if the sounds are in fact spatially non-predictive (i.e., they are as likely to indicate the position of the upcoming target as the opposite location). Lee and Spence subsequently set out to build on this laboratory finding in order to investigate how best to draw a driver's attention to the blind spot (i.e., the region to the rear on the side of the vehicle that cannot be seen via the mirrors) (see also Gruenefeld, Löchen, Brueck, Boll, & Heuten, 2018). They presented spatially non-predictive auditory cues from in front of, or behind, the participant's head on either the left or right (i.e., at 45, 135, 225, and 315° from straight ahead in azimuthal coordinates). However, rather than drawing attention to the cued location (as the laboratory research, all of which had been conducted in frontal space, would have predicted), equivalent cuing effects were seen, no matter whether the auditory cue happened to have been presented from in front or behind on the target side. That is, spatial correspondence seemed to matter along the left-right axis, but not along the front-back axis (though note that spatial hearing is generally more robust in the left-right than front-back axis). In order to understand this surprising result, one really needs to consider the cognitive neuroscience underpinnings of crossmodal attention. In particular, how different regions of space may be represented by different neural substrates (Gross & Graziano, 1995; Previc, 1998; Spence, Lee, & Van der Stoep, 2017, for reviews). Neural representations of front and rear space appear to have different response properties, as documented in studies of attentional orienting, overt responding (i.e., head-turning) and multisensory integration. At the same time, however, one also needs to consider a possible interaction between crossmodal spatial attention and multisensory integration. For, according to the latest research (see Montagne & Zhou, 2018), it turns out that rear auditory stimuli can be often ventriloquized[1] into frontal (i.e., visual) space by concurrently-presented frontal visual stimuli.

Ultimately, our contention in this Element is that basic research on cross-modal attention will benefit from a closer consideration of the attentional demands/limitations faced by those interacting with the real world. At the same time, however, there are also many benefits to the field of applied psychology/human factors research that can emerge, and in some cases already have, from the growing laboratory understanding of crossmodal attention. So, for example, the importance of presenting spatial cues to drivers and other interface operators in different modalities from the same spatial location (or direction) is something that is suggested by a host of cognitive neuroscience research findings (see Spence, 2012, for discussion of this as well as a number of other such examples). However, until recently, spatial co-location (of cues or warnings signals in different modalities) was typically not considered important by human factors researchers. To summarize, we start by reviewing key findings that have emerged from laboratory-based research most often involving auditory and visual stimuli presented in near-frontal space. Thereafter, we open the discussion out by looking at the somewhat different challenges faced by those wanting to implement warning signals and interfaces for drivers, incorporating research that has presented stimuli from other regions of space.

Important themes running through the contemporary literature on crossmodal attention include the distinction between exogenous (or stimulus-driven) and endogenous (or voluntary) attentional control, and between overt and covert orienting (see Spence, 2014, for a review). In the spatial senses, overt orienting occurs when sensory receptors move in order to sample information. For example, the eyes move in order to foveate an item of interest. Meanwhile, haptically exploring an object with the fingertips can be thought of as a form of overt tactile orienting (Gallace & Spence, 2014). Given audition's 360° alerting capacity, overt orienting is less pronounced in this modality (see Heffner & Heffner, 1992a, 1992b; Julesz & Hirsh, 1972). Nevertheless, auditory perception has been reported to be somewhat better in the region in front of the head, and at fixation (Maddox, Pospisil, Stecker, & Lee, 2014; Reisberg, 1978; Spence & Read, 2003; see also Rorden & Driver, 1999). Of course, we do tend to orient our heads towards the source of auditory stimulation, and it turns out that even tactile perception can be enhanced by gazing (either directly or

---

[1] Ventriloquism is one of the most widely-studied examples of multisensory integration (https://www.upf.edu/web/mrg/demos).

indirectly) in the direction of the skin site that is being stimulated (Taylor-Clarke, Kennett, & Haggard, 2002; Tipper et al., 1998; Tipper et al., 2001; see also Naveteur, Honore, & Michael, 2005). So, in a sense, the visual fixation of the apparent source of an environmental stimulus, or event, may be considered a kind of crossmodal overt orienting. That is, overt visual attention can be seen as aligning sensory receptors and facilitating the perception of whatever stimulus, or event, happens to be presented from the direction of gaze. Covert orienting, by contrast, occurs when attention is oriented in the absence of any overt shift of the sensory receptors.

We first review the literature on crossmodal exogenous (or stimulus-driven) attentional capture in the laboratory and thereafter in the real-world context of driving. We then do the same for purely endogenous (or voluntary) attentional orienting. Thereafter, we address the question of how these two forms of attentional control interact, as they most certainly do under most real-world conditions, as, for example, when a driver is attempting to multitask while at the wheel. Finally, we take a brief look at crossmodal attention in terms of the chemical senses, again considering the findings in terms of driving.

2 Exogenous Crossmodal Attention

2.1 Basic Laboratory Findings

Researchers have been studying crossmodal attention in earnest under laboratory conditions since the 1970s, ushered in by Mike Posner's classic studies summarized in his book *Chronometric Explorations of Mind* (see Posner, 1978). Thereafter, studies in both neurologically healthy participants (e.g., Buchtel & Butter, 1988; Dufour, 1999; Mondor & Amirault, 1998; Schmitt, Postma, & de Haan, 2000, 2001; Ward, 1994) as well as in brain-damaged patients (Farah, Wong, Monheit, & Morrow, 1989) went on to investigate crossmodal links in spatial attention. Typically, researchers would present task-irrelevant peripheral auditory cues prior to the onset of peripheral visual targets on either the same or opposite side of central fixation. The participants in such studies were normally required to make speeded detection/discrimination responses to visual targets. The stimulus onset asynchrony (SOA) between the cue and target would often be varied in order to enable the scientists concerned to get some sense of the time course of any crossmodal facilitatory effects that may have been obtained. Oftentimes, significant crossmodal cuing effects lasting for several hundred milliseconds after the onset of the cue, were documented.

Unfortunately, however, many of the early studies in this area failed to rule out non-attentional interpretations for the results obtained. Indeed, alternative explanations for these early findings included the suggestion that cuing benefits in non-orthogonal response tasks might reflect response priming (Simon & Craft, 1970), and/or the possibility of shifts in decisional criteria in those studies that relied on simple speeded detection measures (see Spence & Driver, 1997a). Nevertheless, a growing body of empirical research around the turn of the last century convincingly demonstrated that the presentation of task-irrelevant auditory, visual, or tactile stimuli does indeed lead to a spatially localized and temporally transient shift in the focus of spatial attention to the region around the cue. This attentional shift facilitates the processing of targets seemingly regardless of the modality in which they are presented (be they auditory, visual, or tactile) assuming, that is, that they were presented there shortly after the cue (see Gray, Mohebbi, & Tan, 2009; Hillyard, Störmer, Feng, Martinez, & McDonald, 2016; Lee & Spence, 2018; Spence, Nicholls, Gillespie, & Driver, 1998).

Subsequently, researchers went on to demonstrate that these short-lasting crossmodal facilitatory effects were often followed by a longer-lasting supramodal inhibition of return (IOR) (Klein, 2000; Posner & Cohen, 1984). The suggestion here being that, after the initial orienting to the cued location, the focus of attention shifts away from the initially visited region for some hundreds of milliseconds, leaving behind an inhibitory tag in its wake (see Spence, Lloyd, McGlone, Nicholls, & Driver, 2000). While IOR has primarily been shown to slow speeded detection latencies, it has, on occasion, also been shown to influence discrimination Reaction Times (RTs) too (e.g., Lupiáñez, Milán, Tornay, Madrid, & Tudela, 1998; Pratt & Abrams, 1999). Research by Van der Stoep, Van der Stigchel, Nijboer, & Spence (2017) has shown that IOR can also influence multisensory integration (see also Wang, Yue, & Chen, 2012).

Over the last couple of decades, John McDonald and his colleagues in North America have published a number of studies documenting the genuinely perceptual nature of the improvements in target processing that can be elicited by a covert exogenous crossmodal shift of attention.[2] The majority of their research has focused on what happens to visual perception following the presentation of spatially non-predictive auditory cues (see McDonald, Störmer, Martinez, Feng, & Hillyard, 2013; McDonald, Teder-Sälejärvi, & Hillyard, 2000; McDonald, Whitman, Störmer, & Hillyard, 2014; Ward, McDonald, & Golestani, 1998; and McDonald, Green, Störmer, & Hillyard, 2012; Spence, McDonald, & Driver, 2004, for reviews; though see also Ward, McDonald, &

---

[2] Here, a distinction is drawn by researchers between the RT facilitation effects that have been documented in speeded detection/discrimination tasks, which might simply result from the prior entry of the attended stimulus (see Spence, Shore, & Klein, 2001; Van Wassenhove, Grant, & Poeppel, 2005), and the enhanced perceptual sensitivity that is sometimes seen in unspeeded discrimination/identification tasks (see Watt, 1991).

Lin, 2000). That is, transient cues appear to summon attention to their location despite being spatially uninformative. These improvements have usually been expressed in terms of faster responses and/or higher accuracy and precision in responding to visual targets following the presentation of a spatially coincident auditory cue (see also Bolognini, Frassinetti, Serino, & Làdavas, 2005). There is, though, some question as to the automaticity of crossmodal exogenous orienting following the presentation of spatially uninformative peripheral cues (see also Koeliwijn, Bronkhorst, & Theeuwes, 2009b; Mazza, Turatto, Rossi, & Umiltà, 2007; Santangelo, Belardinelli, & Spence, 2007; Santangelo & Spence, 2007b, 2008a).

Carefully controlled psychophysical research by Lu et al. (2009) has since demonstrated that the presentation of a task-irrelevant auditory cue leads to both stimulus enhancement and the exclusion of external noise (see Lu & Dosher, 1998, 2000). The facilitation of visual performance in this case was measured by means of a Gabor-orientation identification task. A recent study by Ahveninen and colleagues (Ahveninen, Ingalls, Yildirim, Calabro, & Vaina, 2019) has suggested that peripheral auditory cues may promote the inhibition of non-relevant visual locations, rather than improve visual accuracy at the cued locations per se, at least at the relatively large eccentricities tested (of 25 to 35 degrees; see also Spence, Shore, & Klein 2001, on the idea of attention as an inhibitory process). At the same time, however, covert crossmodal exogenous spatial orienting has also been shown to speed-up the perceived time of occurrence of stimuli that are presented at the cued location (McDonald, Teder-Sälejärvi, Di Russo, & Hillyard, 2005; cf. Santangelo & Spence, 2008b; Shore, Spence, & Klein, 2001; Spence et al., 2004). That is, a stimulus appearing on the side where attention has been 'summoned' by a cue presented in either the same or a different sensory modality appears to occur earlier than when the same stimulus is presented from another 'uncued' location (though see also Schneider & Bavelier, 2003).

Cognitive neuroscience studies in this area have involved the analysis of event-related potentials (ERPs) as well as the use of other neuroimaging techniques (e.g., Brang et al., 2015; Feng, Störmer, Martinez, McDonald, & Hillyard, 2014, 2017; Green, Teder-Sälejärvi, & McDonald, 2005; Macaluso, Frith, & Driver, 2002b; Störmer, McDonald, & Hillyard, 2009). These approaches have highlighted the early time course of activation in primary sensory areas as well as in those higher-order association areas associated with the crossmodal cuing of spatial attention by exogenous (i.e., non-predictive) cues (see Störmer, 2019, for a recent review). Meanwhile, the involvement of the parietal cortex in intramodal and crossmodal exogenous visuo-tactile spatial orienting was also suggested by the results of a transcranial magnetic stimulation (TMS) study reported by Chambers, Payne, and Mattingley (2007).

Störmer et al. (2009) reported that lateralized auditory cues resulted in visual stimuli subsequently presented from the same location appearing brighter. What is more, this perceptual effect correlated with the size of the ERP effect in early latency visual components (that is, the amplification of visual ERPs to the target in cued vs. uncued trials). Remarkably, such crossmodal effects have been tracked down to a neural modulation in the visual cortex that apparently starts even before the visual event has been presented (Feng et al., 2017). Supporting such an idea, Brang et al. (2015) observed very short-latency contralateral responses in the primary visual cortex (using electrocorticography, ECoG), after the presentation of spatially lateralized sounds. In summary, spatially specific (or at least lateralized) neural effects are seen both in response to the cue and the upcoming target. It should, however, be borne in mind here that, according to research by Matusz, Retsa, and Murray (2016), the contralateral visual response elicited by the presentation of a lateralized non-predictive auditory cue may be context-dependent (see also Campus, Sandini, Morrone, & Gori, 2017). In particular, these researchers only observed an auditory-evoked contralateral occipital positivity component (250 ms after stimulus onset) when the side on which the auditory stimulus was presented was made unpredictable (and not when it was made predictable).

Störmer, Feng, Martinez, McDonald, and Hillyard (2016) reported that the presentation of a salient sound can also trigger the desynchronization of the contralateral occipital alpha rhythm, a neural marker of active visual processing and visual attention. In an animal electrophysiology study, Lakatos, Chen, O'Connell, Mills, and Schroeder (2007) were able to demonstrate that tactile events on the skin produced phasic modulations in the excitability of neurons in the auditory cortex (see also Schroeder & Lakatos, 2009). This phenomenon, called phase resetting, provides a possible neural mechanism underlying such crossmodal interactions, given that an event in one sensory modality may trigger phasic windows of high sensitivity for stimuli in another modality. Several studies in humans have since followed-up in order to address this mechanism. For instance, Fiebelkorn, Foxe, Butler, and Molholm (2011) used psychophysics in order to sample visual detection performance at small time intervals after the onset of an abrupt sound. In support of the phase reset idea, these researchers reported that visual performance fluctuated in a periodic fashion for a few cycles following the onset of the auditory event. Meanwhile, in a study published the next year, Romei, Gross, and Thut (2012) demonstrated that abrupt sounds produced a ~10Hz cyclical fluctuation in visual cortex excitability as measured with TMS-induced phosphenes.

Mercier et al. (2013) provided additional support for crossmodal phase reset from intracranial recordings in humans using ECoG. The mechanism of phase resetting across sensory modalities seems to provide a powerful mechanistic explanation for fast, short-lived interactions that may potentially underlie crossmodal exogenous attention effects. In some cases, however, the spatial specificity of these phase reset effects remains to be confirmed, given the limitations of the technique, or protocol, used. This is obviously an important point to address, given that the fundamental nature of exogenous spatial attention is spatial selection.

2.2 Crossmodal Exogenous Spatial Attention and Multisensory Integration: Similarities and Differences

Having summarized the basic evidence concerning crossmodal exogenous spatial attention, one debate that should be acknowledged here concerns the exact nature of the relationship between crossmodal attention and multisensory integration. In the case of exogenous crossmodal attention, for example, cuing effects are typically maximal a few hundred milliseconds after the onset of the cue stimulus. By contrast, those who have conducted many of the studies of the time course of various multisensory illusions and/or effects have shown maximal interactions centred on the near-simultaneous presentation of the component unisensory stimuli (see Spence & Ngo, 2012, for a review). However, given that the latency of crossmodal attention effects induced by cues can sometimes be observed to occur very soon after stimulus onset (as demonstrated in those studies that have used temporally precise intracortical measurements; see Lakatos et al., 2007), and that multisensory integration effects sometimes take time to build-up, the boundary between the two phenomena can undoubtedly be blurry (cf. Bolognini et al., 2005; Diederich & Colonius, 2019; Leone & McCourt, 2013; Lu et al., 2009; McDonald, Teder-Sälejärvi, & Ward, 2001; Stevenson, Krueger Fister, Barnett, Nidiffer, & Wallace, 2012). And beyond their somewhat different temporal signatures, there is also a separate debate concerning whether attentional effects precede multisensory integration or operate only after multisensory integration has taken place. Support for the latter suggestion comes from those crossmodal cuing studies demonstrating that exogenous spatial attention is drawn to the ventriloquized location of a sound, thus implying that audiovisual multisensory integration precedes the exogenous crossmodal allocation of spatial attention (see Spence & Driver, 2000; Vroomen, Bertelson, & de Gelder, 2001a, 2001b). In Spence and Driver's study, for example, a spatially unlocalizable auditory cue led to a shift of participants' visual attention to the elevation from which a simultaneously presented visual cue happened to have been presented (either above or below fixation). By contrast, either spatially non-predictive unisensory cue (that is unlocalizable auditory or peripheral visual cue), when presented in isolation, had no such effect. The suggestion here being that the perceived location of the sound was first ventriloquized towards the elevation of the visual cue, before exogenous spatial attentional orienting was directed to the ventriloquized location of the sound. Vroomen and his colleagues obtained similar results (Vroomen et al., 2001a, 2001b).

However, research by Van der Stoep, Van der Stigchel, and Nijboer (2015c) has demonstrated that the multisensory integration of auditory and visual stimuli that is indicated by the violation of the race model (Miller, 1982, 1991) was more pronounced for stimuli presented on the exogenously unattended rather than the attended side.[3] In the latter study, the auditory, visual, and audiovisual targets were presented on the left or right, while a spatially non-predictive auditory cue was presented on the same or opposite side after a cue-target onset asynchrony of 200–250 ms. Taken together, therefore, there may be no simple, or unitary answer, as far as the question of the temporal sequencing of multisensory integration and exogenous attention is concerned. Rather the answer is likely to be task dependent. Of course, as far as the human factors researcher wanting to alert the driver to a danger on the road is concerned, the precise mechanism by which facilitation occurs might not matter as much as the magnitude of the reaction time saving that can be achieved. To put this suggestion in context, Suetomi and Kido (1997) estimated that a 500 millisecond reduction in braking latencies would reduce front-to-rear-end collisions[4] by up to 60 per cent! Unfortunately, the size of the facilitation effects in the laboratory are considerably more modest.

2.3 Keeping Track of Space When Posture Changes

Given the spatial specificity of crossmodal attention cuing effects (see Lee & Spence, 2017; Spence et al., 2004), one of the key empirical questions that has interested researchers in this area has been the extent to which such effects update for any changes in body posture (or receptor alignment), such that the correct environmental location or stimulus is attended, regardless of the modalities that happen to have been stimulated. While, ecologically speaking, this would obviously make sense, computationally speaking, the problem is by no

---

[3] There has, though, been debate among mathematically minded psychologists as to whether facilitation seen in this paradigm reflects the benefits of multisensory integration versus the confounds associated with the modality-switch effect (Otto & Mamassian, 2012), an attentional cost associated with shifting attention from one modality to another (Gondan, Lange, Rösler, & Röder, 2004; Miles, Brown, & Poliakoff, 2011; see also Kreutzfeldt, Stephan, Sturm, Willems, & Koch, 2015; Lukas, Philipp, & Koch, 2010, 2014).

[4] These are the most common type of car accident (see Ho & Spence, 2008).

means a trivial one, given the different frames of reference that are initially used for coding visual (retinotopic), auditory (head-centred with auditory stimuli initially being represented tonotopically), and tactile stimuli (somatotopic; see Driver & Spence, 1998; and Pouget, Deneve, & Duhamel, 2002, 2004, on the computational transformations that may be required).

A large body of neurophysiological data on the topic of receptor misalignment[5] has been reported in the anaesthetized animal preparation (e.g., see Morrell, 1972, 1973; Pöppel, 1973). Subsequently, Populin and Yin (1998, 2002) addressed similar questions while recording from the awake cat. In particular, recordings from bimodal neurons in the Superior Colliculus (SC) have been taken to suggest that multisensory interactions (e.g., between auditory and visual stimuli) are updated in response to various kinds of receptor misalignment. Note here that similar questions have also been addressed in the optic tectum of the barn owl (see Hyde & Knudsen, 2002; Knudsen, 1982). By extension, one might well expect crossmodal links in spatial attention following a change in posture, such as the crossing of a person's hands, or the deviation of eye fixation while maintaining the position of the head, to be similarly updated (cf. Harmening, Orlowski, Ben-Shahar, & Wagner, 2011; Johnen, Wagner, & Gaese, 2001).

The SC, along with the frontal eye fields, constitute part of the brain circuit that controls eye movements, and is also implicated in the exogenous control of covert spatial attention (Bollimunta, Bogadhi, & Krauzlis, 2018; de Haan, Morgan, & Rorden, 2008; Ignashchenkova, Dicke, Haarmeier, & Their, 2004; Kustov & Robinson, 1996; Lovejoy & Krauzlis, 2010; Moore, Armstrong, & Fallah, 2003). The results of laboratory research conducted in neurologically healthy adult humans has revealed that crossmodal links in spatial attention do indeed appear to operate on representations of space that, by and large, update for any such changes in posture (see Driver & Spence, 1998; Kennett, Eimer, Spence, & Driver, 2001; Kennett, Spence, & Driver, 2002).[6] Kennett et al. (2001), for instance, demonstrated that vibrotactile cues presented to the left or right hand led to a facilitation of speeded visual elevation discrimination responses in the same azimuthal location (or side) regardless of whether the participants held their hands in an uncrossed or crossed posture.

Researchers have addressed the time course of these spatial transformations from the native frame of reference in which a stimulus is initially encoded

---

[5] Receptor misalignment refers to the situation in which the receptor arrays for the different senses are misaligned due to a change in posture, such as deviating the eyes with respect to the head, or crossing the hands over while keeping one's eyes open.

[6] Lloyd, Shore, Spence, and Calvert (2003b) highlighted the cortical remapping taking place in posterior parietal cortex in human participants following the crossing of one of their arms over the midline (see also Ora, Wada, Salat, & Kansaku, 2016, for a more recent follow-up additionally highlighting changes in functional connectivity when the hand/arm is crossed over the midline).

through to the common reference frame needed to align spatial representations in terms of external space (this is referred to as spatial remapping). For instance, Azañón and Soto-Faraco (2008a) tracked the time course of the crossmodal cuing of visual attention following the presentation of tactile cues to the hands which were positioned in different postures (with the participants' hands either uncrossed or crossed). For cue-target latencies in excess of 150 ms, crossmodal cuing effects were effectively expressed in terms of external location. That is, posture was compensated for in accordance with previous studies using similar cue-target latencies (Kennett et al., 2001, 2002). Interestingly, however, at shorter cue-target latencies (i.e., up to around 100 ms), crossmodal cuing effects were expressed in terms of anatomical side instead. That is, a tactile cue presented to the left hand facilitated visual targets presented to the left hemi-field, regardless of whether or not the cued left hand was crossed over to the right of the body midline. Such results would therefore appear to suggest that exogenous crossmodal cuing effects operate on updated spatial representations only after some process of remapping has taken place (triggered, presumably, by the presentation of the stimuli themselves).

In a similar vein, Overvliet, Azañón, and Soto-Faraco (2011) assessed speeded saccadic response latencies to tactile events that were presented on their partici-pants' hands, which could, once again, be placed in either their normal straight (i.e., uncrossed) posture or else crossed over the body midline. Whereas, in the 'normal' uncrossed posture, the majority of saccades went straight to the stimu-lated hand, once participants adopted a crossed hands posture, many of the early latency saccades started off towards the wrong side (e.g., the side the hand would have been in the canonical uncrossed body posture), only for this misdirected trajectory to be corrected soon thereafter. Such results therefore provide support for the view that the remapping of tactile stimuli takes around a couple of hundred milliseconds, at least in uncommon postures such as when the hands are crossed (cf. Groh & Sparks, 1996, for similar data in monkeys). Note here also that the somewhat time-consuming process of tactile remapping from one spatial frame of reference to another may help to explain the robust crossed hands temporal processing deficit that has repeatedly been documented in those who are sighted, or else have seen at some point in their development (Röder, Rösler, & Spence, 2004; Shore, Spry, & Spence, 2002; Yamamoto & Kitazawa, 2001). In particular, people often get confused about which hand was stimulated first when making tactile temporal order judgements (TOJs), where one stimulus is presented to either hand, when holding their hands in the crossed posture.

While such studies are indeed impressive in terms of highlighting the updat-ing that occurs when different body postures are adopted, what they do not reveal is how rapidly such updating occurs as people move their bodies through space (though see Azañón & Soto-Faraco, 2008b; Azañón, Stenner, Cardini, & Haggard, 2015). One relevant question to ask here then is whether such transformations (or remappings) occur in real time? Does it take time to update following receptor misalignment, or does such updating perhaps even precede the execution of a given action (whose result is a change in posture)? We are unaware of any research on this question specifically in the world of crossmodal exogenous spatial cuing. However, research using the somewhat-related crossmodal congruency task (see Spence, Pavani, & Driver, 2004; and Spence, Pavani, Maravita, & Holmes, 2004b, for a review; see also Fong, Hui, Fung, Chu, & Wang, 2018, on crossmodal flanker interference) has demonstrated that spatial realignment starts to occur just as soon as a movement towards an object, in this case, a hand movement has been planned (see Brozzoli, Cardinali, Pavani, & Farnè, 2010; Brozzoli, Pavani, Cardinali, Urquizar, Cardinali, & Farnè, 2009).[7]

In the crossmodal congruency task, participants are typically required to make speeded discrimination responses concerning the elevation of vibrotactile targets presented to the thumb or index finger of either hand (see Figure 1).

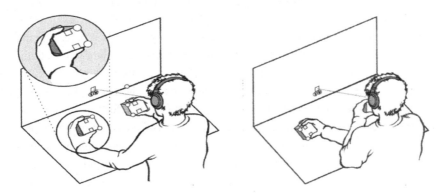

Figure 1 Basic set-up of the crossmodal congruency task. The standard uncrossed posture is shown on the left, the crossed posture on the right. Participants are typically required to make speeded elevation discrimination responses to a series of vibrotactile targets presented to the index finger or thumb of either hand. At the same time, to-be-ignored visual distractors are presented randomly from one of the four possible target locations. [Figure courtesy of Spence et al. (2008).]

---

[7] A separate line of experimental research has demonstrated that tactile (but interestingly not auditory or visual) suppression is observed during the preparatory (i.e., planning) and early stages of movement execution (see Juravle, Binstead, & Spence, 2017, for a review).

At the same time, however, they also have to try and ignore the visual distractor stimulus that is presented from upper or lower locations on the same or opposite side of fixation, near the hands. The crossmodal congruency effect is calculated as the difference in performance (usually RT) as a function of whether the elevation of the visual distractor is congruent or incongruent with that of the target vibration. The onset of the visual distractor is often set to slightly precede that of the vibrotactile target in order to maximize any interference effects that are observed (Shore, Barnes, & Spence, 2006; Spence et al., 2004). Given that robust crossmodal congruence effects have been documented across a range of studies (see Spence, Pavani, Maravita, & Holmes, 2008, for a review; though see also Blustein, Gill, Wilson, & Sensinger, 2019), this has enabled researchers to assess the visuo-tactile representation of space following posture change in both healthy and brain-damaged patients (Spence, Kingstone, Shore, & Gazzaniga, 2001).[8] So, for example, in the two postures shown in Figure 1 (uncrossed and crossed, respectively), visual distractors presented from the same environmental position (i.e., regardless of the participant's posture) have been shown to give rise to the largest crossmodal congruency effect.

The majority of the laboratory research on crossmodal spatial attention that has involved vibrotactile stimuli has restricted their presentation to the finger-tips (see Gallace & Spence, 2014, for a similar observation concerning many other areas of research on tactile perception). One might, therefore, wonder whether similar processes of remapping also occur when, for example, the feet are crossed. This is, by now, a topic that has been investigated in the laboratory, with the results confirming that remapping does indeed take place (e.g., see Badde, Röder, & Heed, 2019; Schicke, Bauer, & Röder, 2009; Schicke & Röder, 2006; van Elk, Forget, & Blanke, 2013). And, more germane to the context of driving, researchers have also been interested in the question of whether tactile remapping occurs as a function of changing eye and/or head orientation when tactile stimuli are presented to the torso instead (e.g., think here only of a vibrating seatbelt or seatback display; cf. Nagel, Carl, Kringe, Märtin, & König, 2005). However, in the latter case, research by Ho and Spence (2007) documented incomplete remapping following the deviation of a participant's gaze. What this means, in practice, is that directional vibrotactile cues are unlikely to direct a driver's visual attention to exactly the right azimuthal location if presented on the torso (e.g., via a vibrating seatbelt) when the driver's overt visual attention is directed away from the straight ahead (e.g., when they

---

[8] Though note that, in the latter case, RTs and accuracy are often combined in a single performance measure known as inverse efficiency.

are looking at one of their wing mirrors, for instance). One is reminded, here, of the fact that while the majority of laboratory research on crossmodal spatial attention has involved static participants with their eyes and head fixed straight ahead (often with any peripherally directed eye movements penalized), the situation while driving likely involves frequent orienting responses (e.g., to check the wing mirrors).

2.4 Crossmodal Attention Outside Near-Frontal Space

The majority of the crossmodal exogenous orienting research that has been reviewed thus far has tended to present auditory, visual, and tactile stimuli from a surprisingly narrow region of near-frontal space (what has some-times been referred to as frontal peripersonal space) (see Figure 2; Van der Stoep, Nijboer, Van der Stigchel, & Spence, 2015; Van der Stoep, Serino, Farnè, Di Luca, & Spence, 2016). This observation then leads on to the obvious (and important) follow-up question of whether the same rules of crossmodal attention (and multisensory integration) identified in the very

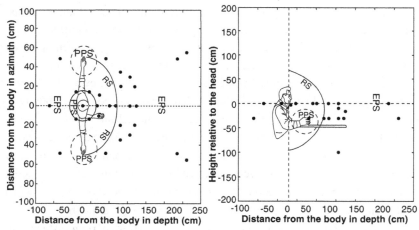

Figure 2 The narrow region of frontal space in which most crossmodal attention research has been conducted. The dots indicate the locations from which the stimuli were presented in a representative selection of 12 studies. Bird's-eye view of the different distances in lateral space and in depth (left panel) and the elevation and depth (right panel) relative to the body (of the participant) from which stimuli have been presented in previous studies of multisensory interactions. PPS = peripersonal space, EPS = extrapersonal space, RS = reachable space. [Figure courtesy of Van der Stoep, Serino, Farnè, Di Luca, & Spence, (2016).]

restricted region of frontal space also apply in other regions of space as well. Reasons to question this assertion come from cognitive neuroscience research demonstrating that the different regions of space around an individual are represented by differentiated brain networks (see Graziano & Gross, 1995; Previc, 1998, for reviews). In fact, this is part of the explanation for why patients with brain damage sometimes exhibit selective difficulties in perceiving and/or responding to stimuli in only certain specific regions of space (e.g., Laeng, Brennen, Johannessen, Holmen, & Elvestad, 2002; Ramachandran, Altschuler, & Hillyer, 1997).

There is, after all, presumably no need to believe that identical principles of multisensory integration and/or sensory weightings are necessarily preserved across different neural representations. Animal electrophysiology studies of multisensory neurons illustrate this point well. Indeed, a common observation in these studies is that spatially tuned multisensory neurons have overlapping visual and auditory (and/or tactile) receptive fields (RFs). However, as the animal moves its eyes about, these representations tend to misalign because visual RFs shift according to the extent of the eye movement whereas the auditory RF only shifts partially, say by 50 per cent of the extent of the eye movement. What is more, the larger the eye movement, the larger the discrepancy between RFs in different modalities (see Pouget et al., 2002, for a review and computational account).

One of the interesting (if seldom addressed) aspects of crossmodal processing is that different modalities cover different regions of space. For example, audition is a 360° sense whereas the visual field covers an area that is approximately 180° wide, with large variations in acuity throughout the field of view. Given the absence of any direct visual contribution to the space behind our own head, it is easy to see how the patterns of sensory dominance (normally visual dominance in frontal space) might be qualitatively different in rear space (see Spence et al., 2017, for a review).[9] Another relevant division of space relates to how far distant events take place from the observer's body. Animal neurophysiology has documented the existence of specific brain representations that appear to be tuned to the processing of stimuli presented from different narrowly constrained regions of space around the animal: Think here only of Graziano and Gross' (1995) impressive work demonstrating that neurons in the so-called polysensory zone (roughly comprising F4 and ventral Premotor Cortex, PMv, of the monkey brain)

---

[9] To give a striking example of how performance can change when the same multisensory task is performed in different regions of space, the crossed hands temporal processing deficit (mentioned earlier) has been shown to disappear entirely when participants cross their hands behind their backs (i.e., in a region of space that has no visual representation) rather than when crossed in front, as is normally the case (see Kóbor, Füredi, Kovács, Spence, & Vidnyánszky, 2006).

appear to be dedicated to detecting auditory and tactile stimuli that originate from just behind the animal's head, thereafter triggering stereotypical orienting and/or defensive responses (e.g., when this area is electrically stimulated) (see Graziano, Gross, Taylor, & Moore, 2004, for a review).

This region, referred to as near-rear peripersonal space, appears to have dedicated neural representations in humans too. At least that is the conclusion of neuropsychological research with hemineglect/extinction patients who are seemingly unable to attend to stimuli presented in a specific (neglected) region of space, despite responding appropriately when the same stimuli are moved into other regions of space (Farnè & Làdavas, 2002; Van der Stoep et al., 2013). In terms of the evidence from neurologically healthy individuals, psychophysical research conducted here at the Crossmodal Research Laboratory, at Oxford University's Department of Experimental Psychology has demonstrated that spatial interactions between auditory and tactile stimuli tend to be easier to observe in near-rear space than when exactly the same stimuli are presented in frontal space instead (e.g., see Kitagawa, Zampini, & Spence, 2005; Occelli, Hartcher-O'Brien, Spence, & Zampini, 2010; Zampini, Torresan, Spence, & Murray, 2007; and Occelli, Spence, & Zampini, 2011, for a review).

For instance, in Kitagawa et al.'s (2005) studies, participants made speeded discrimination responses concerning the side (left vs. right) from which tactile targets were presented. At the same time, however, they had to try and ignore simultaneously presented auditory distractors, which could be presented from either side. Surprisingly, the results revealed no sign of a spatial congruency effect when the auditory and tactile stimuli were presented in frontal space. By contrast, a significant crossmodal congruency effect was observed when the same stimuli were presented from just behind the participant's head instead. Similarly, Occelli and her colleagues have also documented a somewhat different pattern of audio-tactile interactions (in a variant of the Colavita visual dominance paradigm)[10] in front as opposed to near-rear space (Occelli et al., 2010). As we will see below, the discovery of this brain circuit dedicated to monitoring near-rear peripersonal space (and triggering defensive orienting responses) has been incorporated into the design of a novel class of warning signals that elicit more rapid head orienting responses from drivers

---

[10] The term, 'the Colavita effect' was initially used to refer to the finding that people would fail to respond to the auditory stimulus on bimodal audiovisual target trials, in a situation in which the majority of stimuli requiring a speeded response were either unimodal auditory or unimodal visual targets (see Spence, Parise, & Chen, 2011, for a review). Subsequently, researchers have demonstrated similar crossmodal extinction effect for other pairs of sensory modalities as well.

who may be otherwise distracted (see Ashley, 2001; Ho & Spence, 2009; Strayer et al., 2019).

2.5 Differences between Laboratory Research and the Driving Situation

Turning to the applied theme underpinning this particular Element, the driver clearly needs to be able to pay attention to (that is, be aware of) stimuli that are presented at different distances, and in all possible directions around them (after all, dangerous events may originate from any direction while driving). Furthermore, while traditionally the driver's attention would have been restricted to those auditory and visual stimuli signalling objects and events outside the body of the vehicle, the growing use of tactile displays, alerts, and warning signals inside vehicles is increasingly common (as in the lane-deviation butt-shakers (sometimes referred to as buttkickers in gaming) found on either side of a driver's seat; Ho, Reed, & Spence, 2007; see Ho & Spence, 2008, for a review). What this means, in practice, is that drivers also increasingly need to pay attention, as well as respond, to information presented through the tactile channel (see Spence & Driver, 1997b; Spence & Ho, 2008a). Note here that an additional consequence of the increasing use of in-vehicle warning signals (be they tactile or in other sensory modalities) might be an increasing need for drivers to focus their attention inside the vehicle (as opposed to outside).

Consideration of the driving case also highlights the contrast between the passive (and stationary) participant in a typical laboratory study of crossmodal attention and the driver who, while also seated, is likely to be engaged in a considerably more dynamic situation. To start with, the vehicle in which the driver is seated will likely be moving in a specific direction (mostly forward and, very occasionally, backward while reversing). This fact then raises a number of interesting questions concerning how the representation, and prioritization, of different regions of space changes as a function of a constrained range of possible movements/optical flow, and of varying levels of threat/anxiety (e.g., think of what it feels like to drive on a rainy night on the motorway with heavy goods traffic all around you) (Poliakoff, Miles, Li, & Blanchette, 2007; Sambo & Iannetti, 2013; cf. Keil et al., 2007; Koster, Crombez, Van Damme, Verschuere, & De Houwer, 2004).

Relevant here, Noel et al. (2015) have documented that the limits of audio-tactile peripersonal space extend further in front of those participants who are walking forward (on a treadmill) as compared to when they were stationary. In particular, looming sounds that approached the participant from the front were

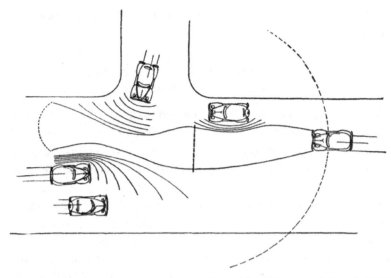

Figure 3 'The zone of safe travel', as envisaged by Gibson and Crooks (1938). [Figure reprinted from Gibson & Crooks, 1938).]

found to facilitate the detection of a vibrotactile target stimulus presented to the chest at a distance of 65–100 cm in the stationary condition. This crossmodal facilitatory effect was documented to occur at a significantly larger distance (1.66 m when they were walking forward; though intriguingly regardless of whether optic flow information was provided).[11]

The driving situation perhaps shares more in common with traditional notions of the body buffer zone (Hediger, 1955; Horowitz, Duff, & Stratton, 1964), and the concept, from ethology, of 'the zone of safe travel'. This is the name given to the space in front of an animal that is prioritized as the route to safe escape (see Spence & Ho, 2008c, for a review). In one of the first studies of driving to have been published, the famous experimental psychologist, J. J. Gibson, working together with an engineer (Gibson & Crooks, 1938), extended this notion of the zone of safe travel to the case of driving (see Figure 3). While we are not aware of anyone having taken-up this concept in subsequent research, the fundamental notion that the representation of different regions of space may change as a function of actual (or potential) action (or for that matter threat) (see Van Damme, Gallace, Spence, Crombez, & Moseley, 2009; and Moseley, Gallace, & Spence, 2012) seems likely to be correct. It is certainly easy to imagine how the region of frontal peripersonal space may

---

[11] Whether moving forward also results in a modification of the distal border of near-rear periper-sonal space is currently unknown.

expand further to the front in someone who is driving (note also the similarities with the notion of peripersonal space extension following tool use) (e.g., Galli, Noel, Canzoneri, Blanke, & Serino, 2015; Witt, Proffitt, & Epstein, 2005; see Spence, 2011b, for a review). It is also interesting here to highlight Moeller, Zoppke, and Frings' (2016) recent observation that people's perception of distance appears to change when sitting in the front seat of a car versus when they are not.[12]

These changes in the representation of different regions of space might bring about important consequences for the driver's multisensory information processing, especially because near and far frontal space have sometimes been shown to operate under rather different rules of crossmodal attention and multisensory integration (note that some of these studies were mentioned earlier, in Section 2.4; see also Serino, Annella, & Avenanti, 2009). Psychophysical studies conducted by Nathan Van der Stoep and his colleagues have shown that this is often the case: So, for example, in one study, Van der Stoep, Van der Stigchel, Nijboer, and Van der Smagt (2016) demonstrated that audiovisual interactions were modulated by whether the relevant auditory and visual stimuli were both presented from near-frontal space, both from far frontal space, or one stimulus was presented from near while the other stimulus was presented from far. Elsewhere, in the case of audiovisual integration, research by Noel, Modi, Wallace, and Van der Stoep (2018; see also Noel, Lukowska, Wallace, & Serino, 2016) supports the notion that the temporal window of audiovisual multisensory integration appears to be wider in near as opposed to far frontal space, while the multisensory response enhancement resulting from bimodal stimulation in the redundant target task does not appear to be affected by distance. Meanwhile, others have reported differences in visual dominance between near and far frontal space (Yue, Jiang, Li, Wang, & Chen, 2015).

There are, of course, also a number of other potentially relevant differences in terms of crossmodal interactions when comparing the actual driving situation versus in the lab, which may affect the distribution of their spatial attention. First, the driver's asymmetric location within the body of the car is worth noting (see Nicholls et al., 2014, for research on this score). Second, the tendency,

---

[12] Of course, one other difference in the case of the driver is that they are separated from what they see and hear on the roadway around them by a transparent barrier (namely the windscreen). While a number of studies have demonstrated that the presence of such a transparent barrier in front of a participant in the laboratory situation significantly impacts the nature of any crossmodal attention and/or multisensory integration effects that are observed (see Kitagawa & Spence, 2005; see also Farnè, Demattè, & Làdavas, 2003, for neuropsychological data from patients suffering from extinction), this has mostly been demonstrated in the context of crossmodal interactions involving the tactile modality. As such, the implications for crossmodal attention in the context of driving, if any, are currently rather less clear.

sometimes commented on in the academic literature, for drivers to incorporate [the vehicle] into their own body representation (see Holmes & Spence, 2005, for a review). Indeed, to the extent that the car becomes incorporated into some kind of extended body representation that might also be expected to bias the distribution of their spatial attention (Yue, Bischof, Zhou, Spence, & Röder, 2009).

A third factor that should be considered here concerns whether there are any passengers in the car. If so, the driver may be operating under conditions of so-called 'social presence' or 'social attention'. A small but growing body of empirical research now shows how performance in various attentional tasks changes as a function of the presence of others, even if that other person happens to be performing a seemingly unrelated task, or perhaps no task at all (e.g., Atmaca, Sebanz, & Knoblich, 2011; Dittrich, Bossert, Rothe-Wulf, & Klauer, 2017; Heed, Habets, Sebanz, & Knoblich, 2010; Nuku & Bekkering, 2010; Risko & Kingstone, 2011; Risko, Richardson, & Kingstone, 2016; Teneggi, Canzoneri, di Pellegrino, & Serino, 2013; Wahn, Keshava, Sinnett, Kingstone, & König, 2017), as is so often the case with a front seat passenger. (Indeed, such findings might give a whole new meaning to the notion of the 'back-seat driver'.) The driver, in other words, often has company, whereas the experimental participant is mostly isolated. Given such differences, it would seem relevant to ask whether the outcomes in terms of crossmodal attention and interactions might be somewhat different too.

2.6 Crossmodal Attentional Capture by Meaningful Stimuli

Another interesting issue that is highlighted by contrasting laboratory with real-world research on the topic of crossmodal attention is the fact that mostly meaningless stimuli have been used in the laboratory studies that have been published to date. That is, researchers have tended to focus on cue stimuli that have no intrinsic motivational/reward value (see Taffou & Viaud-Delmon, 2014). Until recently, simple stimuli such as pure tones, brief flashes of light, and/or brief vibrotactile pulses applied to the fingertips have mostly been used as both the cue and the target stimuli in much of the early crossmodal exogenous spatial attention research (e.g., see the research reviewed in Spence, 2014; Spence & Driver, 2004). This approach with simple stimuli is thought to simplify the interpretation of results, but it is in sharp contrasts with the situation of the warning signals used in driving research (and practice), where iconic stimuli are much more common: Be it the flashing visual icons on the dashboard, or the auditory icons (such as the sound of a car horn or even the screeching of car tyres) (Graham, 1999) recommended in the auditory modality (see Belz, Robinson, & Casali, 1999; Gaver, 1986; Ho & Spence, 2005b; Lucas, 1995). It is by no means clear, a priori, that the results obtained with simple meaningless stimuli will necessarily generalize to more iconic stimuli, some of which may have an enhanced ability to capture our attention because of their relevance/meaning (see Oyer & Hardick, 1963, for early military research on this theme; and Mack & Rock, 1998).

It is also important to note that there are many different visual and potentially also auditory warning signals that the driver might need to respond to while driving (see McKeown & Isherwood, 2007). Furthermore, these warning signals need to be recognizable given that they may only be presented relatively infrequently while at the same time requiring an immediate (i.e., time-critical) response from the driver (see Spence & Ho, 2008b). On top of that, it is important to be sure that the presentation of a rare, or infrequent, warning signal does not itself lead to a startle response which could produce an undesired drop of attention to the road (see Lee, Hoffman, & Hayes, 2004, on the use of graded alerts). Once again, the situation here contrasts in a number of salient ways with that faced by the participant in the typical laboratory study of crossmodal spatial attention. In laboratory studies, one and the same cue stimulus may well be presented 1000 times or more over the course of a 60-minute experimental session (see Spence & Driver, 1997a).[13]

Research on the question of how crossmodal interactions with meaningful, as compared to meaningless, stimuli affects the time course of the distribution of spatial attention while driving is currently scant. There are, however, some research findings emerging from a slightly different situation, namely visual online search for target products (think Amazon search display or doing online shopping) that are potentially relevant. For instance, Knoeferle, Knoeferle, Velasco, and Spence (2016) reported a series of studies showing that the presentation of product-related sounds facilitated the search for congruent products situated in amongst cluttered visual displays. So, for example, in online displays of 12 products, those who were searching for a box of matches found the target significantly faster if the search display was preceded by the sound of a striking match, say. Meanwhile, another of Knoeferle et al.'s studies, in which participants' eye movements were monitored, revealed a similar pattern of crossmodal facilitation in terms of the overt orienting of their visual attention. What was perhaps most remarkable was that sonic logos, or jingles, paired with specific products for the first time at the start of the study, soon started to lead to the same

---

[13] Note that one of the advantages of the one-shot version of the inattention blindness paradigm (e.g., Mack & Rock, 1998), covered later in this Element, is that it tests people's perception of a single stimulus presented without any prior warning, thus making it more obviously applicable to real-life driving contexts than many of the other experimental paradigms described here.

crossmodal orienting benefits, as other well-established crossmodal semantically meaningful mappings.

Other researchers have also reported that the characteristic sound of an object can facilitate a participant's ability to find the image of that object in a visual search task (see Iordanescu, Grabowecky, Franconeri, Theeuwes, & Suzuki, 2010; Iordanescu, Grabowecky, & Suzuki, 2011; Iordanescu, Guzman-Martinez, Grabowecky, & Suzuki, 2008; Kvasova, García-Vernet, & Soto-Faraco, 2019). At the same time, however, research using simple displays to study the facilitatory crossmodal effect of the verbal presentation of the name of the object, or a distinctive object sound (think of the pop of a champagne cork), have demonstrated that such meaningful crossmodal facilitation effects take time, and are perhaps better considered in terms of crossmodal priming, rather than necessarily as a form of multisensory integration (see Chen & Spence, 2013; and see Amado et al., 2018; Battistoni, Kaiser, Hickey, & Peelen, 2018, for functional neuroimaging research on such cross-domain priming).[14] By analogy with the product-sound related research reported by Knoeferle et al. (2016) and others, one might consider whether the sound of a bicycle bell could be used to prime drivers to pay more attention to any cyclist in among cluttered visual road scenes, say (cf. Ho, Hollingworth, Hollingworth, & Spence, 2015, unpublished, on the importance of increasing the driver's awareness of such 'vulnerable' road users). The sound of a car's horn, meanwhile would presumably attract visual attention to any other cars that are visible (see also Wu, Wick, & Pomplun, 2014).

Separate from the literature of crossmodal attentional facilitation by semantically meaningful auditory cues, there have also been a number of studies demonstrating that crossmodal correspondences can be used to bias people's visual search behaviour. Crossmodal correspondences have been defined as the associations that people experience between features, attributes, or dimensions of experience in different sensory modalities, either physically present or else when merely imagined (see Spence, 2011a, for a review). In recent decades, crossmodal correspondences have been shown to bias people's behaviour across a range of tasks. Relevant to the present context, auditory cues have been used to prioritize the visual search for those stimuli that correspond in some way with the pitch of the sound (see Chiou & Rich, 2012; Klapetek, Ngo, & Spence, 2012; Orchard-Mills, Alais, & Van der Burg, 2013a, b). So, for instance, both Orchard-Mills, Van der Burg, and Alais, (2016) and Chiou and

---

[14]   Remember here that as we saw earlier, one feature of multisensory integration effects is that they tend to be maximal when the inputs are simultaneous (see also Spence & Ngo, 2012, for a review and critical assessment).

Rich demonstrated that the presentation of a non-predictive central auditory cue that was either relatively low or high in pitch exogenously directed their participants' attention in the elevation dimension (see Spence, 2019a, on the relative nature of many crossmodal correspondences). Specifically, the presentation of a task-irrelevant low-pitched auditory cue led to a short-lasting shift of attention downwards, whereas the presentation of a relatively high-pitched auditory cue resulted in an upward shift of attention instead (though see Klein, Brennan, & Gilani, 1987, for early null results using a very similar approach).

Elsewhere, Klapetek and her colleagues demonstrated that their participants' ability to discriminate the orientation of a horizontal or vertical line segment presented in among multiple other tilted distractors in a challenging visual search task was significantly better when the pitch of a synchronized auditory cue matched the lightness of the visual target (Klapetek et al., 2012; see also Van der Burg, Olivers, Bronkhorst, & Theeuwes, 2008a; Zou, Müller, & Shi, 2012). However, the crossmodal correspondence between the pitch of the spatially uninformative target-synchronous sound and the brightness of the visual target only facilitated performance when the participants were made aware of the underpinning correspondence. This and other results have subsequently been taken to suggest that crossmodal attentional effects that are based on crossmodal correspondences are not truly automatic given that they can sometimes be over-ridden and may, on occasion, need to be established first (see also Getz & Kubovy, 2018; Orchard-Mills et al., 2013a; Spence & Deroy, 2013).

Various applied studies have assessed the potentially beneficial effect of presenting co-localized auditory and, on occasion, tactile cues on participants' ability to localize visual targets presented somewhere in 3D space (e.g., Perrott, Saberi, Brown, & Strybel, 1990; Perrott, Sadralodabai, Saberi, & Strybel, 1991; Rudmann & Strybel, 1999; see also Hancock et al., 2015; Hancock, Mercado, Merlo, & Van Erp, 2013; Hopkins, Kass, Blalock, & Brill, 2017; Merlo & Hancock, 2011). The latter have often been presented using either individua-lized or generic Head-Related Transfer Functions (HRTFs) in order to make headphone-presented sounds appear to have originated from a particular posi-tion in 3D space (e.g., Begault & Pittman, 1996; Perrott, Cisneros, McKinley, & D'Angelo, 1996; Soret, Hurter, & Peysakhovich, 2019). Thus far, this kind of 360° crossmodal facilitation has primarily been of interest in the context of aviation (i.e., when trying to guide the visual attention of a pilot), but it might be worth considering its potential use in driving, too (see Fitch, Kiefer, Hankey, & Kleiner, 2007, for a simplified prototype). That said, as Fitch et al. found in their study, the problem in the closed reflective confines of the car's interior is that drivers often find it hard to localize sounds correctly.

One other class of biologically relevant stimuli are looming signals. Indeed, auditory and visual looming signals have been shown to provide a particularly effective means of capturing people's attention (both crossmodally as well as intramodally) in laboratory situations (e.g., Cléry, Guipponi, Odouard, Wardak, & Ben Hamed, 2015; Lee & Spence, 2018; Leo, Romei, Freeman, Ladavas, & Driver, 2011). However, here in Oxford, our own attempts to deliver tactile looming signals via the torso have so far proved less than impressive (Ho, Spence, & Gray, 2013; though see Meng, Ho, Gray, & Spence, 2015a, 2015b; Meng & Spence, 2015, for a slightly different approach). Indeed, this disappointing result should probably not come as much of a surprise to those familiar with the difficulty that human factors researchers have long faced when trying to develop tactile stimuli that are in any meaningful sense, iconic (i.e., like the sound of the car horn in audition) (e.g., Brewster & Brown, 2004; Chan, MacLean, & McGrenere, 2005).

Another class of attention-directing, meaningful cues are verbal stimuli such as the spoken words 'front' or 'back', 'left' or 'right' (see Baldwin, 2011; Edworthy & Hellier, 2006). According to one definition, these should be considered as symbolic cues that require an observer to set in motion the (slower) voluntary orienting system, rather than the automatic exogenous orienting system. However, the research suggests that verbal cues can elicit a seemingly automatic shift of spatial attention in the direction indicated by the word cue (see Ho & Spence, 2006). One practical limitation associated with the use of such verbal cues is that they require the driver to understand the language in which they are presented (something that might not always be the case) – contrast this, once again, with the intuitively meaningful sound of the car horn.[15] Regarding the question of how cues can effectively engage fast spatial orienting in drivers, there is also uncertainty concerning the frame of reference that will be adopted when a verbal command 'left' or 'right' occurs in the context of a sensorimotor visual task (Castro, Soto-Faraco, Morís-Fernández, & Ruzzoli, 2018; Ruzzoli & Soto-Faraco, 2017).[16]

Across the various semantically meaningful warning signals that have been reviewed in this section, there is something of an unresolved issue as to whether the cue, or warning signal, directs attention to the location of its source, or to whatever the meaning of the stimulus refers, or relates to. To put this

---

[15] However, even if the driver does speak the right language, one might need to test whether cues presented in a non-native tongue can produce orienting as effectively (and quickly) as in the case of an individual's first language. We are not aware of any laboratory-based research addressing this question.

[16] After all, is someone who is facing us head on were to say 'It's on the left', it would be ambiguous whose left they were talking about.

uncertainty concretely, imagine yourself hearing a warning signal on your right barking out the word 'left'. Will attention exogenously be drawn to the location from which that auditory cue is presented, only for it to be redirected 'automatically' (?) in the direction indicated by the meaning of the word? As yet, we simply do not have the answer to this question (see Wogalter, Kalsher, & Racicot, 1993). This, then, is just one of the knowledge lacunae resulting from the limited focus of laboratory-based research on a limited range of simplistic, meaningless cue stimuli without much consideration of the applied context in which such warning signals might be presented. Here, it is possible that the context in which the signal is presented may play a role. It is certainly easy to imagine how if, for example, the location of the sound varies from one trial to the next, this may help to make it relevant to the participant, in a way that it is not if the location from which a sound is presented is fixed (see Matusz et al., 2016; Zampini, Guest, Shore, & Spence, 2005, on this theme).

2.7 Integrating the Response Modality into Crossmodal Attention Research

Another important factor that has been neglected by much of the laboratory-based crossmodal attention research concerns the actions that may be required when responding to a given imperative signal (cf. Baumeister, Vohs, & Funder, 2007; Engel, Maye, Kurthen, & König, 2013; Zmigrod, Spapé, & Hommel, 2009). In the laboratory, this might reflect the fact that most of the time researchers have primarily been interested in the perceptual components of the effects that they study, and hence have wanted to disregard any response-related components. In fact, laboratory researchers interested in perceptual effects mostly tend to treat the response element as nothing more than a confound, one that is to be avoided wherever possible. The majority of laboratory-based studies have used button-press responses using protocols specifically designed to minimize the contribution of motor influences to the effects under investigation and so hone in purely crossmodal perceptual attentional effects (i.e., and so rule out potential response biases). The implicit assumption here among researchers would seem to have been that the nature of the response (modality), and/or response effector doesn't really have any meaningful impact on the crossmodal attentional phenomena under study, whatever they might be, and hence can be safely ignored. Other psychophysicists, meanwhile, have wanted to go further and dismiss speeded responses entirely (see Watt, 1991, p. 213, for one particularly fervent suggestion along these lines), advocating the use of unspeeded perceptual judgments instead.

However, a quick consideration of the situation while driving immediately brings home the fact that (unspeeded) button-pressing constitutes only a very small proportion/subset of the actions that a driver needs to perform and, what is more, few safety-critical driving tasks require such a response. While driving, attentional orienting and action are inevitably conflated. In our own research here at the Crossmodal Research Laboratory in Oxford, for example, much of the last 15 years have been spent investigating the ability of auditory and tactile cues to direct a driver's attention exogenously towards either the front or back. A response-related 'confound' has thus run through much of our research. For, in the driving context, if something happens on the roadway ahead then more often than not it means that a braking response will be required from the driver. By contrast, if a vehicle accelerates from behind, then the natural tendency is to try and accelerate away from it. In other words, the direction in which attention is directed and the response that is required, are often correlated in the real world. In one study, though, we were able to dissociate the influence of spatial attention from the priming of the appropriate motor response (braking or accelerating) by having our participants make a speeded discrimination response concerning the colour of the number plate seen on the car in front (through the virtual windscreen) or behind (seen via the rear-view mirror) (see Ho & Spence, 2008; Ho, Tan, & Spence, 2006). In this case, our results revealed that while the magnitude of the crossmodal benefits were maximal when the position of the sound (or tactile stimulus from the front or back) primed the relevant response, a significant crossmodal cuing effect was nevertheless still observed even when the participants had to discriminate the colour of the number plate, and so response priming could be eliminated as an explanation for any response facilitation observed (see Figure 4).

Several studies from the laboratory have also demonstrated that various (crossmodal) attentional phenomena are affected by the response effectors used (see Ho & Spence, 2014) and by the response modality (Gallace, Soto-Faraco, Dalton, Kreukniet, & Spence, 2008; see also Azañón, Camacho, & Soto-Faraco, 2010). Illustrating the impact of response modality on crossmodal attentional phenomena, Azañón et al. reported that crossmodal exogenous attentional effects were substantially attenuated when their participants had to respond verbally rather than via foot pedals, despite the actual cue-target protocol being exactly the same in both cases. Such results therefore hint at the importance of the specific response that an individual will likely need to execute as being a relevant factor as, for example, when designing an attention-capturing warning signal for drivers or any other kind of interface operator. Note that this is especially likely to be true for those situations that require a particular speeded response to a given imperative signal.

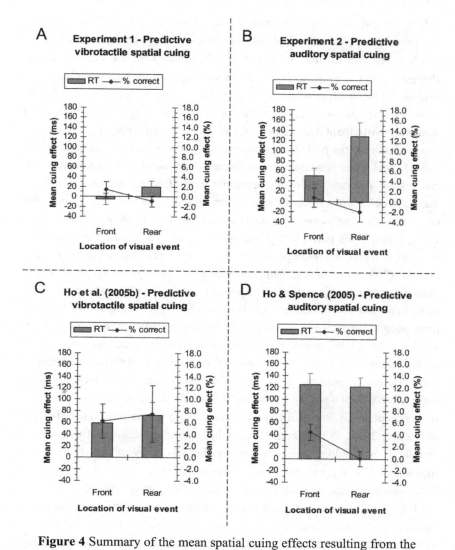

Figure 4 Summary of the mean spatial cuing effects resulting from the presentation of spatially-predictive vibrotactile (Ho et al., 2006, Experiment 1) and auditory (Ho et al., 2006, Experiment 2) cues from the front or rear (Panels A and B, respectively), spatially predictive vibrotactile cuing in Ho, Tan, and Spence's (2005b) study (C) and spatially predictive auditory cuing in Ho and Spence's (2005b) study (D). RT = reaction times. The error bars show the standard errors of the means. The results in the upper panels were from studies in which participants had to discriminate the changing colour of the number plate (either red or green) of the car seen on the road in front or behind, while the results in the lower panels show the benefits on driver braking/accelerating latencies. The larger cuing effects reported in the lower panels presumably

It is also worth stressing here the fact that the average driver makes numerous different bodily movements while in charge of their vehicle (i.e., moving their feet for the foot pedals and their hands for the steering wheel, changing gears in a manual car, and interacting with various other displays/ controls). The situation while driving, in other words, is really quite different from the one that is typically instantiated in laboratory studies where the stationary participant does not move, and where the only response/movement that is allowed is the periodic manual pressing of one or other response key. In order to make this consideration of the response modality/type concrete, we can take a relevant real-world example here. Earlier, we mentioned the orienting/defensive responses that are triggered by electrically stimulating neurons in the polysensory zone (F4/PMv) in the monkey (see Graziano et al., 2004). This part of the brain has been shown to selectively process auditory and tactile stimuli presented in near-rear peripersonal space. Ho and Spence (2009) took these neurophysiological findings as inspiration and demonstrated that if the desired response from the driver was a rapid head-turn, then this overt orienting response could be triggered most effectively by presenting a lateralized broadband noise from just behind the driver's head (c. 20–70 cm away). When exactly the same sound was presented from a different region of space the benefits (in terms of the facilitation of response latencies) were not as pronounced. However, if the appropriate behavioural response were to have been a simple button press instead (i.e., rather than a head-turn) then, speculatively, such a difference would likely not have been seen (cf. Ho & Spence, 2014, on this theme). Note that a similar criticism of personality and social psychology research, namely that too many of the studies have focused on self-reports and finger movements rather than studying actual behaviour, has been forcefully made by Baumeister et al. (2007).

Finally in this section, it is worth noting how a person's attention appears to be drawn to the space around their own limbs (e.g., Abrams, Davoli, Du, Knapp, & Paull, 2008; Dufour & Touzalin, 2008; Hari & Jousmäki, 1996; Michael

---

Caption for Figure 4 (cont.)

reflect the beneficial effects of attentional facilitation and response priming, whereas the reduced cuing effects shown in the upper panels reflect solely the impact of attentional facilitation. Note here also how auditory cues tend to give rise to larger cuing benefits than vibrotactile cues. Intriguingly, however, this modality difference disappears if the auditory cues are brought closer to the driver's body. [Figure reprinted with permission from Ho et al. (2006).]

et al., 2012; Reed, Grubb, & Steele, 2006; see also Weidler & Abrams, 2014).[17] In the context of driving, therefore, one might wonder how the driver's attention is distributed spatially given that their hands are often likely to be in full view, outstretched on the steering wheel (cf. Streicher & Estes, 2016, on the impact of grasping on visual search behaviour). Of course, when playing ball sports, for example, our attention is presumably directed towards the ball/any action that is taking place on the pitch rather than to our hands. As such, the most appropriate conclusion to draw from the laboratory studies may well only be that attention tends to be directed to the peri-hand region when there is nothing else more exciting going on in the scene. Of course, this is rarely likely to be the case when driving.

2.8 Capturing Attention Exogenously Using Multisensory Cues

Earlier we saw how Van der Stoep, Van der Stigchel, & Nijboer, (2015) assessed the impact of exogenous attention on people's speeded responses to auditory, visual, and audiovisual target stimuli. Here, we briefly want to look at those studies that have attempted to determine whether exogenous spatial attention is captured more effectively by spatially non-predictive multisensory cues than by unisensory cues. Relevant early research here comes from Spence and Driver (1999). These researchers assessed the impact of combined audiovisual cues in a version of the orthogonal spatial cuing paradigm, described earlier (cf. Spence & Driver, 1997a). Specifically, auditory and visual cues were presented from the same peripheral location on either the left or right. However, contrary to expectations, there was little evidence that multisensory cues captured people's spatial attention any more effectively than unisensory cues. Note that a similar conclusion has also been reached by those researchers who have assessed exogenous orienting under conditions where the participant has no other task to perform than simply to respond to target stimuli presented every few seconds (Santangelo et al., 2007; though see also Van der Burg, Olivers, Bronkhorst, & Theeuwes, 2008b).

As we will see later, though, the situation changes completely as soon as the participant is engaged in an attention-demanding task (Santangelo & Spence, 2007a; though see also Matusz & Eimer, 2011, 2013; van der Lubbe & Postma, 2005).[18] Looking to the future, one of the intriguing

---

[17] Elsewhere, neuropsychological data from di Pellegrino, Làdavas, and Farné (1997) has illustrated that the neglect of tactile events on the hand could be elicited by the presentation of competing visual stimuli that were presented near the contralateral hand, but that these same competing visual events did not produce tactile neglect if presented away from the body.

[18] Separate from the multisensory cuing literature using meaningless auditory and visual cues, research by Conrad et al. (2013) has demonstrated that biologically-relevant multisensory stimuli can be especially effective at capturing our attention. In particular, these researchers

questions in crossmodal attention research currently is the speed at which people learn novel associations between otherwise-unrelated stimuli in different sensory modalities, and how this then facilitates the spread of attention crossmodally from one sense to the other (see Baier, Kleinschmidt, & Müller, 2006; Busse, Roberts, Crist, Weissman, & Woldorff, 2005; Fiebelkorn, Foxe, & Molholm, 2010, 2012; Turatto, Mazza, & Umiltà, 2005; Zangenehpour & Zatorre, 2010). In passing here, one might also wonder whether pairs of associated stimuli would be any more (or less) likely to capture a person's attention.

2.9 Interim Summary

The research that has been reviewed in this section clearly highlights the existence of robust (if not necessarily always automatic) crossmodal links in exogenous spatial attention between audition, vision, and touch. While the majority of this research has been conducted in a relatively narrow region of frontal space (see Van der Stoep, Serino, Farnè, Di Luca, & Spence, 2016, for a review) there is evidence to suggest that exogenous crossmodal links in spatial attention also exist in other regions of space as well. However, the precise nature of the links between attention in the different senses also appears to differ as a function of the particular region of space in which the stimuli have been presented. At the same time, however, the research also makes clear the need to consider the response demands of the task as a relevant factor, something that has been largely downplayed in laboratory research on crossmodal attention to date. Importantly, throughout this section, a number of salient differences between the research that has been conducted in the laboratory, using simple and largely meaningless stimuli presented to isolated participants in sensorially impoverished contexts, and the real-life situations such as driving have been highlighted (see also Juan et al., 2017). In the case of driving, the range of attention-capturing signals that are presented tends to be much wider than typically incorporated in laboratory studies. What is more, individual warning signals tend to be semantically meaningful, too. While the cognitive neuroscientists have mostly focused their efforts on trying to understand the neural mechanisms underlying audiovisual crossmodal exogenous attention in near-frontal space, the human factors researchers have been far more interested in figuring out the best way in which to capture people's attention and elicit the appropriate behavioural response, for stimuli/events that might occur from pretty much any direction in 3D-space.

---

investigated audiovisual looming signals (see also Cappe, Thelen, Romei, Thut, & Murray, 2012; Orioli, Bremner, & Farroni, 2018).

3 Endogenous Crossmodal Attention

3.1 Basic Laboratory Findings

Just as for the case of crossmodal exogenous attentional orienting, discussed so far, extensive crossmodal links have also been reported in the case of covert endogenous orienting (e.g., see Doruk et al., 2018; Driver & Spence, 2004; Lloyd, Merat, McGlone, & Spence, 2003; Spence & Driver, 1996; Spence, Lloyd, et al., 2000). Several studies conducted over the last couple of decades have revealed clear signs of ERP modulations in response to stimuli in one sensory modality, as a function of endogenous spatial attention shifts in another (e.g., Eimer, 2004; Eimer, Cockburn, Smedley, & Driver, 2001; Eimer & Driver, 2001; Eimer, Van Velzen, & Driver, 2004; Green, Doesburg, Ward, & McDonald, 2011). Some of these studies have also revealed signs of anticipatory processes mostly reflected in posterior, as well as anterior electrode locations, following the presentation of a spatial cue in one modality, and crucially before the target had been presented in another. The consequences of these shifts in spatial attention have revealed early crossmodal effects in ERP responses, and modulations in the blood-oxygen level dependent (BOLD) response in modality-specific brain areas (using functional magnetic resonance imaging, fMRI) (Macaluso, Frith, & Driver, 2000).

In terms of the neural substrates underlying any crossmodal links in endogenous spatial attention, parietal areas known to maintain a representation of space appear to play an important role (e.g., see Chambers, Stokes, & Mattingley, 2004; Kida et al., 2007). Put simply, the majority of the results that have been published to date are more consistent with the 'separable-but-linked' hypothesis (as originally suggested by Spence & Driver, 1996; see also Spence, 2010b). Of course, endogenous attention may be directed to a location or to a specific sensory modality. The neural mechanisms underlying the crossmodal shifting/focusing of attention from one sensory modality to another have also been studied quite extensively (Bauer, Kennett, & Driver, 2012; Hairston et al., 2008; Mühlberg, Oriolo, & Soto-Faraco, 2014; Mühlberg & Soto-Faraco, 2018). So, for instance, reduced brain activity in unattended modalities has been reported in various neuroimaging studies (Bauer et al., 2012; Keil, Pomper, & Senkowski, 2016; Macaluso, Frith, & Driver, 2002a; Mozolic et al., 2008; Pomper, Keil, Foxe, & Senkowski, 2015). Supporting this idea, the results of a number of studies suggest that modality-specific brain areas corresponding to task irrelevant sensory modalities tend to be suppressed via low-frequency oscillatory activity when attention is selectively directed to a task-relevant modality (Keil et al., 2016; Pomper et al., 2015). For example, magnetoencephalography (MEG) research by Bauer et al. (2012) suggests that low-frequency oscillations may help to up- or down-regulate the excitability of neural representations in the sensory cortices that are associated with the attended/unattended modality (respectively). Furthermore, according to Bauer et al., this regulatory mechanism could act on spatial, as well as modality-based selection (the latter, a topic we will return to later). Taken together, therefore, the evidence would appear to support the conclusion that just as for the case of exogenous orienting, there are extensive crossmodal constraints on the endogenous control of spatial attention as well.

Here, it is important to note that while directing attention to one sensory modality or another does not always enhance behavioural performance, presenting stimuli in a modality that has been actively inhibited (i.e., unattended) does appear to impair performance, be it in a spatial attention or discrimination task, or even an unspeeded perceptual task (see also Johnson, Strafella, & Zatorre, 2007; Johnson & Zatorre, 2006; Kawashima, O'Sullivan, & Roland, 1995; Shomstein & Yantis, 2004; Spence, Nicholls, & Driver, 2001; Spence, Shore, & Klein, 2001, for a review).[19] Finally here, it should be borne in mind that differences between the perceptual consequences/neural signatures associated with attending to a sensory modality versus spatial location have been reported (Spence, Shore, & Klein, 2001; Vibell, Klinge, Zampini, Nobre, & Spence, 2017; Vibell, Klinge, Zampini, Spence, & Nobre, 2007).[20] But what, one might ask, do such fundamental findings from the lab have to do with driving?

3.2 Crossmodal Endogenous Spatial Attention in Driving

Drivers often try to direct their auditory and visual attention in different directions simultaneously. However, people find it difficult to divide their endogenous attention spatially under laboratory conditions (e.g., see Driver & Spence, 1994; Eimer, 1999; Hillyard, Simpson, Woods, Van Voorhis, & Münte, 1984; Posner, 1990; Spence & Driver, 1996; Spence, Ranson, & Driver, 2000; though see Alais, Morrone, & Burr, 2006; Soto-Faraco, Morein-Zamir, & Kingstone, 2005). What is more, exactly the same constraints on dividing/focusing endogenous spatial attention have also been demonstrated when participants respond to any particular combination of auditory, tactile, and visual target stimuli (see Lloyd, Merat, McGlone, & Spence, 2003, on audio-tactile, and Spence, Pavani, & Driver,

---

[19] Although beyond the scope of the present Element, it should also be noted here that attention can also be directed to a modality exogenously (see Spence, Kettenmann, Kobal, & McGlone, 2001a; Turatto, Benso, Galfano, Gamberini, & Umiltà, 2002; Turatto, Galfano, Bridgeman, & Umiltà, 2004).

[20] And, although we do not have time to look at it, it is worth noting that there has been a lot of research on the orienting of attention in time, and there is a crossmodal angle there too (e.g., see Lange & Röder, 2006).

2000, on visuo-tactile endogenous spatial attention; and see Driver & Spence, 2004, for a review). Specifically, the participants in numerous laboratory studies have been shown to find it easier to simultaneously attend to audition and touch in the same location, while finding it harder to divide their attention to different spatial locations. On the flip side, however, people tend to find it more difficult to ignore auditory stimuli at the location they are attending visually, while finding it easier to ignore if auditory distractors are presented from a different location from the one where tactile attention is directed (cf. Kahneman & Treisman, 1984).

To address the question of whether dividing the focus of attention spatially in different sensory modalities is also particularly difficult while driving, Spence and Read (2003) conducted a study at the University of Leeds driving simulator. Their participants (all experienced drivers, it should be noted) had to constantly repeat back one of two simultaneously presented speech streams while trying to ignore the other. One speech stream, consisting of triplets of bi-syllabic words, was presented from directly in front of the driver/participant while the other one was presented from the passenger side. Background noise was added from a central location in order to make the shadowing task more difficult. The participants were either parked in a stationary situation in a car, and so only performed the shadowing task (the single-task condition), or else were required to drive along a challenging inner-city road network while shadowing (the dual-task condition). The manipulation of experimental interest was whether or not the relevant auditory stream was presented from the same direction as visual attention (both overtly and covertly) was focused (i.e., directly ahead out of the front of the windscreen on the road ahead).

In line with the majority of the laboratory-based research, the participants' shadowing performance under dual-task conditions was significantly better when the auditory stimuli were presented from the presumed direction of participants' visual attention (i.e., straight ahead). At the same time, however, it should also be borne in mind here that the cost of dividing attention spatially was only seen on the shadowing task, not in terms of driving performance. The suggestion here, as in many other studies of this type, being that Spence and Read's (2003) participants presumably prioritized safe driving over shadowing. Future research should perhaps address whether under more challenging driving conditions (or when engaged in a more stimulating conversation than just repeating back lists of words presented in background noise), the trade-off between safe driving and speaking might break down (see Strayer & Johnston, 2001). Nevertheless, these results do, we would argue, potentially have implications for those human factors researchers wanting to optimize the layout of their information displays and interfaces (see also Kunar, Carter, Cohen, & Horowitz, 2008).

3.3 Divided Attention and the Multiple Resource Theory

Traditionally, one of the major concerns of human factors researchers was with people talking on the phone while at the wheel (e.g., McEvoy, Stevenson, & Woodward, 2007a; Patten, Kircher, Ostlund, & Nilsson, 2004). Increasingly, though, the issue nowadays is with all those drivers who text while driving, unaware of the dangers they are putting themselves (not to mention their passengers and other road users) in. Regarding the issue of talking (on the phone) while driving, according to traditional models of attention, such as Wickens' Multiple Resource Theory or MRT (see Wickens, 1984, 1992, 2002; see also Hancock, Oron-Gilad, & Szalma, 2007; Sarter, 2007), the human operator has separate pools of resources for the processing of auditory and visual information, and therefore attention can be efficiently divided between modalities. According to MRT, the human operator also has separate resources for the processing of spatial and verbal information, and for manual vs. vocal responding (see Figure 5).[21]

Although somewhat disconnected from the latest laboratory research findings on crossmodal attention (see below), it is worth noting that the MRT approach has been hugely influential in the field of human factors for several decades now. According to the MRT framework, there should not be any crossmodal

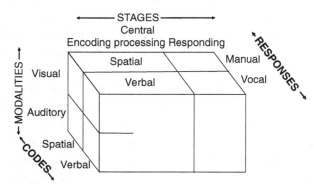

Figure 5 Separable pools of information processing resources, according to Wickens (1984, 1992, 2002). Note the clear distinction between auditory and visual processing resources. Subsequently, researchers have also added a pool of tactile processing resources as well (see text for details). This has been the dominant model in the field of human factors/ergonomics research for the last 40 years.

---

[21] Subsequently, researchers have recognized the need to add a pool of tactile resources (e.g., Lu, Wickens, Sarter, & Sebok, 2011; Scerra & Brill, 2012).

attentional constraints on maintaining a conversation while driving,[22] since talking uses auditory, verbal, and vocal resources, whereas driving is primarily a visual, spatial, manual endeavour (see Senders, Kristofferson, Levison, Dietrich, & Ward, 1967; Sivak, 1996). Potentially relevant neuroimaging data here have demonstrated a reduction in activity in those brain areas related to functions that are thought to be critical for driving (e.g., visuospatial and attentional activity associated with parietal areas) when people lying in the brain scanner were simultaneously required to listen to someone speaking (Just, Kellar, & Cynkar, 2008).[23] Such results certainly suggest the view that processing resources are shared between the modalities, rather than being entirely separate, as Wickens would have us believe (see Lennie, 2003, on a possible neural account of resources).

A large and robust body of epidemiological data has demonstrated that, presumably because talking decreases attention to driving (Ho & Spence, 2008, chapter 2), the risk of having an accident increases fourfold in those who have just been using their phone (Redelmeier & Tibshirani, 1997). Early commentators were often tempted to point to the possible manipulation problems associated with holding a mobile phone while driving. However, the emergence of hands-free devices has not had a significant impact on accident rates (see Ho & Spence, 2008, for a review). Rather, the difficulty of talking while driving would appear to concern more the allocation of central resources related to attention (Strayer, Drews, & Johnston, 2003). In fact, inattention is cited as a leading cause of accidents on the roads, accounting for somewhere between, a quarter and a little over a half of all road traffic accidents (see Brown, 2001; see Ho & Spence, 2008, for a review).

Horrey and Wickens (2006) attempted to account for such seemingly damning evidence (both epidemiological and neuroimaging) within the constraints of the MRT approach. One of their suggestions was that the resources involved in driving and speaking are not entirely separate. Rather, they suggested, under conditions that are sufficiently demanding, some resources may be transferred from one resource pool to another. They also pointed to the fact that the MRT approach was principally designed to account for/predict the difficulties that people experience when dividing attention in continuous monitoring tasks, rather than in those situations in which speeded responses to discrete events

---

[22] While, a priori, talking to a passenger might seem no different from talking to someone on a mobile device, the research shows the latter to be significantly more demanding of attention (e.g., see Amado & Ulupinar, 2005; McEvoy, Stevenson, & Woodward, 2007b).

[23] According to a recent review by Palmiero et al. (2019), when a secondary task is added while driving, neuronal resources are redirected away from visual processing, i.e., a shift in activation is seen from occipital to fronto-parietal brain regions.

are required (as is arguably the case while responding in an emergency braking situation while driving, say). Several groups of cognitive neuroscientists (e.g., Talsma, Doty, Strowd, & Woldorff, 2006; Wahn & König, 2016, 2017) have reported that there appears to be a more extensive pool of attentional resources across the senses than when tasks are combined within a sense (see Section 3.4 for more on this theme). Taken together, therefore, the growing literature in this area would not seem to be entirely compatible with either a pure modality-specific account nor with an account exclusively in terms of a unitary (i.e., common) pool of resources.

3.4 Perceptual Load and Crossmodal Attention

Laboratory-based researchers have also long been interested in the question of whether people have access to various different modality-specific pools of processing resources for perception or instead have just a single shared pool of resources for the processing of all incoming sensory information (see Lavie, 1995, 2005, 2010; and Murphy, Spence, & Dalton, 2017, for a review of the literature on perceptual load in audition; though see Benoni & Tsal, 2010, 2013; Tsal & Benoni, 2010, for a critical appraisal). The concept of 'perceptual load' refers to the number of different items that are relevant (potentially needed to perform the task) and/or the amount of resources required for the perceptual identification of those items. This approach is often used to account for the potential of sudden irrelevant events to capture attention while a person is focused on some primary task or other. Early research (Rees, Frith, & Lavie, 2001; Tellinghuisen & Nowak, 2003) tended to converge on the view that the effects of increasing perceptual load were indeed modality-specific (as implied by MRT, and as suggested by some of the early cognitive psychology studies, e.g., Shiffrin & Grantham, 1974; Treisman & Davies, 1973, on which Wickens' model was based). However, as we have just seen, subsequent studies have demonstrated that loading one sensory modality sometimes impacts on the attentional processing that is seen in another (e.g., see Berman & Colby, 2002; Ciaramitaro, Chow, & Eglington, 2017; Dehais, Causse, Vachon, Régis, Menant, & Tremblay, 2014; Houghton, Macken, & Jones, 2003; Molloy, Griffiths, Chait, & Lavie, 2015; Murphy & Greene, 2017; Otten, Alain, & Picton, 2000; Parks, Hilimire, & Corballis, 2009; Sinnett, Costa, & Soto-Faraco, 2006; Wahn & König, 2015a, 2015b; see Murphy, Dalton, & Spence, 2017, for a review).

In one such representative study, Ciaramitaro et al. (2017) documented an enhanced auditory sensitivity (for both amplitude- and frequency-modulated sounds) in a two-interval forced choice design when their participants were instructed to perform a less (as compared to a more) demanding visual task. The visual task in this case involved the monitoring of a Rapid Serial Visual Presentation (RSVP) stream for the interval in which the stream contained a particular colour (low load) or else, in separate blocks of trials, the interval containing more of a particular target letter. Ciaramitaro et al.'s results therefore suggest that increasing the demands of a visual task can influence the processing of auditory information on an unrelated concurrent task, thus providing support for the claim that attentional resources are shared between the senses.

Support for the shared resources view also comes from a study by Wahn and König (2016) in which the participants had to perform a visual search task and either a vibrotactile or visual localization task. As might have been expected, considerable interference between the two tasks was documented. However, the participants performed the visual search task more rapidly when engaged in the tactile localization task (the tactile stimuli presented by means of a vibrating display presented to the torso) than when both tasks utilized the same pool of visual attentional resources. These results therefore provide support for the notion that attentional selection for the processing of visual and tactile information is somewhat independent. However, despite the publication of a number of such convincing results, there still continues to be controversy concerning when exactly crossmodal constraints on attention will be observed following the manipulation of perceptual load. For instance, Sandhu and Dyson (2016) failed to demonstrate any crossmodal perceptual load effects associated with the performance of either visual or auditory focal tasks (see also Alais et al., 2006; Arrighi, Lunardi, & Burr, 2011, for other results supporting the separable resources account; and see Jacoby, Hall, & Mattingley, 2012). Meanwhile, Murphy and Dalton (2016) reported a study demonstrating that increasing visual load (in a visual search task) induced tactile inattention (as demonstrated by a lowering of tactile sensitivity in a detection task).

Given such a mixed bag of results, it is currently rather difficult to discern what may be the critical factor determining when exactly performance will lead to the suggestion that resources are shared. Certainly, there would seem to be something task-specific about the interaction. In fact, one of the factors that often turns out to be crucial is that the component tasks are, in some sense, spatial. Indeed, given recent findings showing that the visual cortex is recruited when participants perform a spatial auditory task, this might be the shared resources that may help to explain crossmodal interference (Campus et al., 2017). Relevant here, then, are findings from Wahn and König (2015a, 2015b) showing interference in the audiovisual and visuo-tactile case when spatial tasks were involved in both modalities.

3.5 Time-Locked Crossmodal Deficits in Dual-Task Performance

One especially important aspect of attention in relation to driving relates to temporary declines in reacting to a given stimulus right after another attentionally demanding event has been processed. As far as the requirement to make multiple speeded responses to stimuli presented in different sensory modalities in rapid succession is concerned, one needs to consider the extensive body of research on the Psychological Refractory Period (PRP) (Welford, 1952; see also Spence, 2008). According to Hal Pashler, who has worked extensively on such tasks, the PRP can be thought of as a time-locked limitation in making speeded responses to different stimuli/tasks within a short time-window. Crucially for present purposes, this dual-task bottleneck in response selection would appear to be insensitive to the modalities (i.e., same versus different) in which the imperative signals are presented (see Pashler, 1994, 1992). The central bottleneck can, in some sense, be considered to be 'amodal' (cf. Arnell, 2006; Potter, Chun, Banks, & Muckenhoupt, 1998). Especially relevant to the themes of the present Element, a PRP effect has been reported in the context of a simulated driving task conducted in the laboratory. In particular, Levy, Pashler, and Boer (2006) demonstrated that having their participants make a speeded manual/ vocal discrimination response to either an auditory or visual imperative signal temporarily impaired their subsequent performance in braking in response to the appearance of the brake lights in a car seen in front. Results such as this suggest that there is a bottleneck somewhere between the initial detection of the stimulus and motor reaction, which seems to have an effect across many information processing domains.

In recent decades, though, the notion that there is a fixed (i.e., unavoidable) bottleneck in human information processing, as Pashler and others would have us believe, has come under increasing pressure from the academic community. In large part, this is because a growing number of researchers now believe that this particular bottleneck may reflect more of a strategic response to the specific demands of the PRP paradigm than a fixed bottleneck in human information processing. Specifically, critics of the PRP approach have drawn attention to the rather contrived situation in which one task is always presented at the same time or very shortly after the other task-relevant stimulus (see Miller, Ulrich, & Rolke, 2009; Schumacher et al., 2001, on this theme), with both imperative target stimuli requiring a speeded response.

The story with regards to other (hypothetical) central attentional bottlenecks, such as tapped by the so-called attentional blink (AB) (e.g., Raymond, Shapiro, &

Arnell, 1992) remains rather more uncertain. The AB refers to the phenomenon that the second of two target events cannot be detected or identified when it appears close in time after the first. While in many ways similar to the PRP bottleneck, the AB can also be observed in unspeeded tasks, and hence appears to reflect more of an attentional/perceptual limitation, than necessarily a limit on response selection. In recent decades, robust intramodal ABs have been demonstrated in the visual, auditory, and on occasion, tactile modalities (see Dell'Acqua, Jolicoeur, Pesciarelli, Job, & Palomba, 2003; Dell'Acqua, Jolicoeur, Sessa, & Turatto, 2006; Hillstrom, Shapiro, & Spence, 2002; Soto-Faraco & Spence, 2002). However, demonstrating a reliable crossmodal AB has proved far more elusive. That is not to say that a crossmodal AB has never been reported. Indeed it has, at least under a certain restricted subset of experimental conditions (e.g., Arnell & Jenkins, 2004; Arnell & Larson, 2002; Dell'Acqua, Turatto, & Jolicoeur, 2001; Hein, Parr, & Duncan, 2006; Jolicoeur, 1999; Soto-Faraco et al., 2002). At the same time, however, other researchers have argued that the AB bottleneck is modality-specific instead (e.g., Duncan, Martens, & Ward, 1997; Soto-Faraco & Spence, 2002; Van der Burg, Olivers, Bronkhorst, Koelewijn, & Theeuwes, 2007).

Our sense is that many of the researchers formerly working on this problem (the present authors included) have largely given up on trying to figure out what exactly is going on (i.e., what are the critical factors determining when exactly a crossmodal AB will be observed – though the critical role played by target masking, which operates differently in the different senses, might be relevant here) and simply moved onto other hopefully more tractable topics/questions concerning crossmodal attentional selection. At the same time, however, one might also wonder (especially given the driving-related theme of the present Element) whether the precise situations in which time-locked processing defi-cits such as the AB and PRP occur are likely to be found in real life (Kasper, Cecotti, Touryan, Eckstein, & Giesbrecht, 2014). If they are relatively likely, then it might be very important to address them in depth, given the dramatic consequences that fleeting lapses in attention and/or response preparation could have on the road. However, to the extent that they are not, these central processing limitations may then ultimately turn out to be of rather more theoretical than necessarily practical interest.

3.6 Endogenous Attention and Multisensory Integration

Returning now to the question of whether attention modulates multisensory integration or vice versa, we can now consider the issue once again, but this time from the standpoint of endogenous, rather than exogenous, spatial attention. Indeed, a broad body of empirical research has attempted to address this very question though, it must be said, that not all of the findings necessarily tell a consistent story (see, for instance, the recent special issue on the topic, Hartcher-O'Brien, Soto-Faraco, & Adams, 2017; see also De Meo, Murray, Clarke, & Matusz, 2015; Macaluso et al., 2016; Navarra, Alsius, Soto-Faraco, & Spence, 2009). The interested reader is directed to one of the many reviews on this topic for details of the various arguments/evidence that have been put forward. Put simply, perhaps the most parsimonious conclusion to draw at the present time is that endogenous attention and multisensory integration are capable of influencing one another in multiple ways (e.g., see Fairhall & Macaluso, 2009; Koelewijn, Bronkhorst, & Theeuwes, 2010; Spence, 2018; Talsma, Senkowski, Soto-Faraco, & Woldorff, 2010; Talsma & Woldorff, 2005; though see also Röder & Büchel, 2009).

A number of studies have shown that the outcome of multisensory integration can, under certain circumstances at least, be regulated (or modulated) as a function of whether or not the multisensory stimuli happen to be attended endogenously (e.g., Alsius, Navarra, Campbell, & Soto-Faraco, 2005; Alsius, Möttönen, Sams, Soto-Faraco, & Tiippana, 2014; Alsius, Navarra, & Soto-Faraco, 2007; Gibney et al., 2017; Jensen, Merz, Spence, & Frings, 2019; Moris-Fernández, Visser, Ventura-Campos, Ávila, & Soto-Faraco, 2015; Talsma, Doty, & Woldorff, 2007).[24] At the same time, however, other researchers have shown that the outcome of multisensory integration can itself facilitate endogenous attentional selection (e.g., Driver, 1996; Soto-Faraco, Navarra, & Alsius, 2004; though see also Jack, O'Shea, Cottrell, & Ritter, 2013). There would, though, appear to be an important distinction to be drawn here. On the one hand, instructional manipulations of endogenous attention have typically not been found to exert a significant influence over multisensory integration (e.g., Bertelson, Vroomen, de Gelder, & Driver, 2000; though see also Sanabria, Soto-Faraco, & Spence, 2007). By contrast, a significant modulation of multisensory integration has often been reported by those using perceptual load manipulations of their participants' endogenous attentional resources instead (Eramudugolla, Kamke, Soto-Faraco, & Mattingley, 2011).

As a general comment, looking to the future, it would seem that progress in this field can perhaps best be made by fixing on certain specific questions, and

---

[24] Though it is perhaps worth noting here that some authors seem a little too happy to jump from the observation that attention modulates multisensory integration to the much stronger claim that attention is necessary for integration. Just take the following from the abstract of Gibney et al. (2017): 'Consistent with prior studies, we found that increased perceptual load led to decreased reports of the McGurk illusion, thus confirming the necessity of attention for the integration of speech stimuli'.

asking whether or not the operation of specific types of attention (e.g., exogenous or endogenous; covert vs. overt; load-based vs. instructional manipulations) precede, or follow, specific types, or situations, of multisensory integration (see Soto-Faraco et al., 2019, on this very theme). So, for instance, one specific question about the relative timing (or sequence) of endogenous crossmodal attention and multisensory integration occurs when thinking about the topic of optimal multisensory integration. It turns out that a growing number of phenomena within the field of multisensory integration research are now coming to be understood in terms of maximum likelihood estimation (e.g., Alais & Burr, 2004; Andersen, Tiippana, & Sams, 2004, 2005; Ernst & Banks, 2002; though see also Battaglia, Jacobs, & Aslin, 2003) and the broader framework of Bayesian optimal integration (e.g., Ernst, 2012; Ernst & Bülthoff, 2004; Wozny, Beierholm, & Shams, 2008). The evidence from various studies would appear to imply that optimal Bayesian integration is not influenced by experimental manipulations of endogenous attention, typically achieved by means of secondary visual task loading (e.g., see Helbig & Ernst, 2008; Odegaard, Wozny, & Shams, 2016; Wahn & König, 2016).

One of the differences between endogenous attention and multisensory integration that Chen and Spence (2017) highlighted recently concerns the hemispheric asymmetry in the endogenous control of spatial attention. Specifically, according to attention researchers (and particularly those neuropsychologists studying patients with neglect/extinction; see also Szczepanski & Kastner, 2013), the suggestion is that the right hemisphere directs attention to both sides of space, whereas the left hemisphere only pays attention to the contralateral right side. As such, there is something of an attentional bias, such that stimuli presented on the right side of space are preferentially attended in the neurologically healthy observer when compared to those that are presented on the left, especially under conditions of load (see Thomas & Flew, 2016; and Chen & Spence, 2017, for a summary of the supporting evidence). By contrast, no such asymmetry has been proposed by those working in the field of multisensory integration research (see Stein & Meredith, 1993, for a review). Intriguingly, Chen and Spence were able to support this distinction by presenting the analysis (or reanalysis) of several published studies highlighting just such a performance asymmetry under various experimental conditions. What this means, in practice, is that one can potentially distinguish behaviourally between the operation of attention and multisensory integration. And, more speculatively, in the context of driving, one might reasonably want to consider whether it is better to have one's attention preferentially directed towards oncoming traffic (as here in the UK where we drive on the left, and hence see oncoming traffic in our right visual field) or instead focused preferentially on what might be occurring on the roadside (as in the rest of the world where the cars drive on the right hand side of the road). Presumably, cross-national accident data, with appropriate controls, might yield some relevant insights here.

3.7 Interim Summary

The research reported in this section has highlighted the fact that there are numerous crossmodal constraints on human information processing. On the one hand, spatial links in endogenous attention mean that people (including drivers) find it more difficult to voluntarily direct their attention in different senses in different directions simultaneously. On the other hand, dual-task studies using a variety of experimental paradigms have revealed the existence of both tonic and phasic dual-task costs associated with trying to process information in different sensory modalities. However, while robust evidence of shared resources for the processing of visual, auditory, and tactile stimuli have been documented in a number of situations, seemingly modality-independent constraints on information processing have been reported in a number of others. While it is currently unclear what the key factor was that distinguished shared vs. separate resources, one factor that has been suggested to play a role is the specific task involved. To the extent that any generalizations are possible, it would appear that spatial tasks are more likely to tap shared resources than are non-spatial tasks. Having reviewed the crossmodal literature on endogenous attention, we next take a look at how endogenous and exogenous attention interact crossmodally as they presumably mostly always do in daily life, and especially when driving.

4 Interactions between Endogenous and Exogenous Attention

4.1 Separating Exogenous from Endogenous Crossmodal Attentional Orienting

As seen in Sections 2 and 3, the majority of the laboratory research on attention (both intramodal and crossmodal) has tended to try and isolate exogenous from endogenous orienting, better to study them individually (see Jonides, 1981; Mueller & Rabbitt, 1989; Spence & Driver, 1996). This behavioural distinction has subsequently been backed-up by functional neuroimaging research suggesting that endogenous and exogenous orienting are underpinned by distinct yet partially overlapping neural circuitry (e.g., Buschman & Miller, 2007; Chica, Bartolomeo, & Lupiáñez, 2013; Corbetta & Shulman, 2002; Santangelo, Olivetti Belardinelli, Spence, & Macaluso, 2009). Interestingly, some commentators have wanted to conceptualize endogenous and exogenous orienting in terms of different ways of shifting the same underlying pool of attentional resources to better process those stimuli that may be of particular interest to the organism (Berger, Henik, & Rafal, 2005). However, according to another line of thought, the behavioural, perceptual, and neural consequences of orienting attention exogenously versus endogenously are actually really quite different, at least in certain respects (e.g., see Carrasco, 2011; Prinzmetal, McCool, & Park, 2005; Prinzmetal, Park, & Garrett, 2005; see also Briand & Klein, 1987).

4.2 Interactions between Exogenous and Endogenous Orienting

Of course, while theoretically meaningful, those situations in which exogenous or endogenous mechanisms of attention are isolated do bear rather little relation to the real world, where the voluntary and involuntary mechanisms (or control) of attention are normally in a state of constant interaction (e.g., see Ho & Spence, 2005b; Serences et al., 2005). It is perhaps fortuitous, therefore, that having spent so many years trying to keep them separate, a number of behavioural researchers have, in recent years, started to consider how these two forms of crossmodal attention (or control, in general) interact (e.g., Blurton, Greenlee, & Gondan, 2015; Chen, Chen, Gao, & Yue, 2012; Chiou & Rich, 2012; Klein et al., 1987; Koelewijn et al., 2009b; Li, Chen, Han, Chui, & Wu, 2012; Spence & Driver, 1994, 2004; Tang, Wu, & Shen, 2016). Once again, though, the results of this research have by no means always proved simple to explain/interpret. One line of research on the interaction between exogenous and endogenous attention has involved the presentation of peripheral cues that were made predictive of either the same or opposite target location (Chica, Sanabria, Lupiáñez, & Spence, 2007; Chiou & Rich, 2012; Klein et al., 1987; Spence & Driver, 1994). Under such conditions, the largest spatial cuing effects are nearly always seen when endogenous and exogenous attention are in alignment (that is, when the location of the peripheral cue indicates the likely location of the target). When, however, they are set in conflict, an initial exogenous cuing effect directed towards the cued location is normally soon overridden by the slower-acting endogenous system.

It is interesting here to consider how, in the context of driving, warning signals fit certain of the attributes of exogenous cues (e.g., being unpredictable, abrupt, and salient). At the same time, however, they will often bear some symbolic association about what the driver should be attending to and/or doing. As such, the presentation of a warning signal likely also triggers endogenous orienting as the driver attempts to interpret the meaning of the cue/warning signal that has just caught their attention exogenously (see Ahtamad, Gray, Ho,

Reed, & Spence, 2015). Given that it takes time to redirect one's attention endogenously to a location that is different from the one where the cue has been presented, there are obviously grounds for wanting to locate the warning signal in the direction that the driver's attention should be drawn towards (see also Proctor & Vu, 2016; Simon, 1990, on the design of compatible warnings and alerts in the context of interface design).

Other laboratory researchers, meanwhile, have combined multiple sequentially presented cues that again might coincide or diverge in terms of where they draw a participant's attention to, either exogenously or endogenously. So, for instance, Koelewijn et al. (2009b) had their participants perform a speeded visual elevation discrimination task on either the left or right. Peripheral auditory and visual cues were both found to exogenously capture their participants' spatial attention when they were non-predictive with regards to the likely target location. When, however, the visual cues were made 80 per cent predictive with regard to the likely target location in a subsequent experiment, auditory capture was no longer observed. By contrast, when the auditory cue was made predictive of the target location in a third study, visual capture was still observed. Meanwhile, Chen et al. (2012) have also documented some asymmetries in the interaction of exogenous and endogenous orienting in the case of auditory and visual attention. While we do not have the space to go into such results in any detail, taken together, they do appear to suggest that the role played by these two modalities (audition and vision) in terms of capturing/ directing attention is by no means interchangeable (see also Prime, McDonald, Green, & Ward, 2008; Spence & Driver, 1994; Ward, 1994, on the much older literature on crossmodal asymmetries in the case of audiovisual exogenous orienting).

4.3 Capturing the Attention of a Distracted Driver

A second approach to the study of the interaction between endogenous and exogenous orienting comes from those studies that have assessed the impact of voluntarily performing a primary attention-demanding task in one modality on the capacity of cues presented in another sensory modality to capture exogenous attention (e.g., see Koelewijn, Bronkhorst, & Theeuwes, 2009a; see also Richard et al., 2002; Santangelo & Spence, 2008a; van der Lubbe & Postma, 2005; Wu, Li, Bai, & Touge, 2009). In our own laboratory and driving-simulator research (see Ho & Spence, 2008, for a review), we have been able to compare the benefits, in terms of reduced braking latencies (a good thing when responding to an emergency event), that are associated with the presentation of non-predictive spatial cues with the same cues when the location of the cue is made predictive of the likely location of an event in the roadway around the driver (e.g., see Ho & Spence, 2005b). Generally speaking, the results of a number of such comparisons have shown enhanced cuing benefits in the case of predictive cuing.

For example, the participants in Molloy et al.'s (2015) combined behavioural and MEG study, performed either a high or low perceptual load visual search task while a task-irrelevant sound was presented (at 10 dB above threshold). Auditory-evoked activity in the superior temporal sulcus and posterior middle temporal gyrus was reduced in the high-, as compared to the low-load, condition. Furthermore, a suppressed later-occurring P3 response (putatively related to awareness of the auditory event) was also documented. Meanwhile, a subsequent psychophysical study also revealed reduced awareness judging from the reports about the presence of the sounds, in similar high visual perceptual load conditions (see also Wahn, Murali, Sinnett, & König 2017). The results of this study, then, highlight the existence of a time-locked cross-modal limit in attention. In a way, one can also think of this as similar to the Colavita visual dominance effect that has been studied by researchers for half a century now (see Hirst, Cragg, & Allen, 2018; Spence et al., 2011, for reviews). Such results presumably also provide one explanation for why peripheral auditory cues might not have captured attention under those conditions where endogenous visual attention was focused on a central attention-demanding task. Intriguingly, studies of inattentional blindness have shown that people appear blind, deaf, and numb to stimuli that would normally be noticed, when their attention is intensely focused on some other task (e.g., MacDonald & Lavie, 2011; Mack & Rock, 1998; Sinnett, Costa, & Soto-Faraco, 2006). The perceptual load approach outlined earlier (see Lavie, 2010, for a review) provides one way of thinking about potential distractions in visual attention while driving. According to Lavie's suggestion, the potential for a task-irrelevant event to distract a person from his/her current attentional focus decreases, as the perceptual load of the central (viz. relevant) task increases.

One of the main reasons why warning signals are needed to capture the attention of drivers is that their mental resources may be focused on some other aspect of driving (or else simply distracted), while a new hazard appears on the road (e.g., see Lin & Hsu, 2010; Lu et al., 2013). The rapid disengagement of attention from the previous task and the reorienting of attention to the upcoming event is likely going to be critical in these situations. More generally, the situation of the multitasking driver raises questions about the crossmodal constraints on divided attention. Having highlighted a number of both phasic and tonic difficulties associated with endogenously trying to perform two tasks in different sensory modalities simultaneously, we end by looking at the inter-action between endogenous and exogenous attentional control. As noted earlier, the majority of the laboratory-based research on crossmodal spatial attention has been conducted under simple single-task conditions. By contrast, in the case of warning signals while driving, one really needs warning signals that will still capture a driver's attention even when they are performing one or more other tasks that will likely be consuming many of their attentional resources and/or giving rise to a high perceptual load.

Having recognized the fact that Warning signals and alerts are often needed to capture and redirect a driver's spatial attention while they are engaged in some task that is secondary to driving, such as, for example, checking their email or texting. Looking back at the majority of the early studies of cross-modal covert exogenous orienting (i.e., the studies reviewed in Section 2) it turns out that these studies were nearly always conducted under conditions where no other distraction or task was present. The applied research in this area shows that unisensory auditory and tactile warning signals lose some, if not all, of their ability to capture attention under conditions where drivers/participants are performing an engaging task (e.g., Mohebbi, Gray, & Tan, 2009; see also Carlander, Eriksson, & Oskarsson, 2007). This result connects well with the literature on perceptual load, discussed a moment ago, and suggests that attention capture while focusing on a conversation (auditory modality) can perhaps be better triggered by salient events in another mod-ality. That said, the capacity to do so depends on the need to focus attention on the conversation.

Hopkins et al. (2017) demonstrated that the beneficial effect of presenting spatially informative, lateralized auditory and tactile cues indicating the side on which a visual target (an oriented line segment in a complex visual search display) was presented, was not much reduced under those conditions in which the participant performed a secondary auditory task. Notice here, though, how in contrast to other studies in this area, the cue was spatially predictive (hence likely engaging endogenous as well as exogenous orienting mechanisms). Meanwhile, research by Santangelo, Finoia, Raffone, Olivetti Belardinelli, and Spence (2008) demonstrated that while manipulations of perceptual load affect exogenous spatial orienting, manipulations of working memory load apparently do not (see also Dalton, Lavie, & Spence, 2009; Dalton, Santangelo, & Spence, 2009; Santangelo & Spence, 2007c; Zimmer & Macaluso, 2007).

Across a number of studies, Valerio Santangelo, and his colleagues have been able to demonstrate that the need to monitor a centrally-presented RSVP or a Rapid Serial Auditory Presentation (RSAP) stream for occasionally

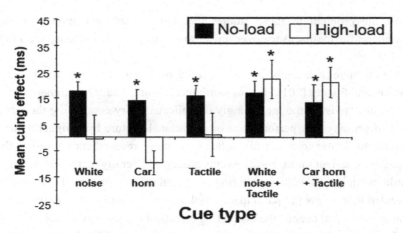

Figure 6 Spatially non-predictive bimodal audio-tactile cues exogenously capture spatial attention regardless of perceptual load, whereas unisensory auditory or tactile cues do not. Notice here how both unisensory and multisensory cues capture attention equally effectively under conditions of low visual load, while only spatially co-located multisensory cues retain their ability to automatically capture exogenous attention under conditions of high visual load (in this case, monitoring an RSVP stream for pre-specified target letters). Asterisk indicates that the mean cuing effect was significantly greater than 0 ($p < .05$). [Modified figure reprinted courtesy of Ho, Santangelo, & Spence, 2009.]

presented targets effectively eliminates the exogenous covert attentional capture by auditory, visual, and/or tactile stimuli (see Santangelo et al., 2007; Santangelo & Spence, 2007b; see also Oray, Lu, & Dawson, 2002; see Santangelo & Spence, 2008a, for a review). However, multisensory audiovisual or audio-tactile cues bypass this limitation, capturing attention just as effectively, and seemingly automatically, regardless of whether or not participants are performing an attention-demanding central task (see Santangelo, Ho, & Spence, 2008; Santangelo & Spence, 2007a; see Spence & Santangelo, 2009, for a review; see Figure 6).[25] Subsequent research by Ho, Santangelo, and Spence (2009) has demonstrated that auditory and tactile component signals needed to be presented from the same direction (if not necessarily the same position) in order to automatically capture attention in this way. Note here how the failure to present the component signals from the same location is

---

[25] Santangelo and Spence (2007a) also demonstrated that double visual cues did not capture participants' attention under conditions of high perceptual load, thus suggesting that there may indeed be something special about multisensory cues.

often the problem in those studies that have failed to demonstrate any advantage for multisensory over unisensory cuing situations (e.g., see Fitch et al., 2007).

Finally here, a recently published study by Lunn, Sjoblom, Ward, Soto-Faraco, and Forster (2019) is also worth mentioning. These researchers added yet another twist to the increasingly complicated story concerning the influence of primary task performance on attentional capture by peripheral cues. Similar to Santangelo and his colleagues, these researchers measured the capacity of salient multisensory events presented laterally to attract attention, while participants were monitoring a central RSVP stream. Their results revealed that unless the participants' task demands required top-down attention to peripheral events, the distracting effects of multisensory cues declined with perceptual load just as much as unisensory ones. Such results might therefore be taken to confirm the close links that exists between endogenous attention and multisensory integration, as discussed in Section 3.6 (see references to recent reviews therein). It is worth noting that in these studies (Santangelo and colleagues, as well as in Lunn et al., 2019), the peripheral auditory and visual stimuli were not presented from exactly the same eccentricity (with visual cues presented from either side of a monitor screen, and auditory cues presented from speakers attached to the side of the monitor, just a few centimetres away). Hence, despite the fact that one could make the argument that exact co-location is necessary for multisensory stimuli to overcome the limitation imposed by high perceptual load (see Spence et al., 2004, for a review of the importance of spatial co-location), it is still true that top-down attention seems to make a difference under the conditions tested by both Santangelo and Spence (2007a) and Lunn et al. (2019). Indeed, Ho et al. (2009) demonstrated explicitly that bimodal audio-tactile cues only break through when presented from the same direction, but not when presented from markedly different directions (though in this case, the disparity between crossmodal inputs was larger with auditory cues presented centrally from a monitor speaker and lateralized cues presented to participant's flanks). It is undoubtedly important to consider the spatio-temporal coincidence of the stimuli, as this can often provide an explanation for why multisensory cuing may not always be any more effective than unisensory cues (see also Chan & Chan, 2006).

Taken together, the majority of the laboratory-based evidence that has been published recently does appear to suggest that multisensory signals (especially when presented from more or less the same direction) exhibit an enhanced capacity to summon attention. While this might reflect nothing more than the added attentional-capturing effects of each unisensory component of the multisensory event (Pápai, 2017; Pápai & Soto-Faraco, 2017), there might also be something special (attentionally speaking) about a multisensory event. The notion of being 'set' for unisensory or multisensory events may also be worth perusing here (i.e., can one be attentionally set for unisensory or for multisensory events?) (see Jensen, Merz, Spence, & Frings, 2020; Mast, Frings, & Spence, 2017). Whatever the most appropriate explanation(s) for the special role that multisensory events can sometimes play, there can be no doubting the widespread growth of interest in multisensory warning signals in the human factors/ergonomics field (e.g., Biondi, Strayer, Rossi, Gastaldi, & Mulatti, 2017; Ho, Spence, & Tan, 2005a; Merlo, Duley, & Hancock, 2010; Oskarsson, Eriksson, & Carlander, 2012; Pjetermeijer, Bazilinskyy, Bengler, & de Winter, 2017).[26]

4.4 Interim Summary

Taken together, the results that have been reported in this section highlight the ongoing interplay between voluntary and automatic control of attention that is typical of daily life situations such as driving. The putatively informative warning signals that are designed to capture the attention of the driver will likely capture attention exogenously before endogenous mechanisms kick in. The other major focus for research in this area concerns the ability of warning signals to exogenously capture the attention of a participant, or more importantly driver, who may be otherwise distracted texting, or else otherwise engaged with their in-car technology (see Ashley, 2001; Ho & Spence, 2008). The remarkable result to emerge from a number of the laboratory studies has been the finding that supposed automatically attention-capturing unisensory auditory, visual, and tactile peripheral cues fail to capture attention when the participant is engaged in a highly attention-demanding task (Santangelo, Ho, & Spence, 2008; Santangelo & Spence, 2007a; see Santangelo & Spence, 2008a; Spence, 2010b, for reviews). Multisensory cues/warning signals, at least when they happen to be presented from approximately the same direction, appear to retain their attention-capturing ability (Ho et al., 2009) (though some results suggest that the multisensory events may need to receive some top-down selection, see Lunn et al., 2019). Returning to a theme that has run through this Element, notice also here how work on attentional capture under high-load conditions also feeds into the debate about whether or not multisensory integration can occur outside the focus of attention.

---

[26] Here, though, it is important to remember not to overload a driver with too many different warning signals (see Biondi, Leo, Gastaldi, Rossi, & Mulatti, 2016).

5 Olfactory Contributions to Crossmodal Attention While Driving

Thus far, the focus of this Element has been squarely on studying crossmodal attention in the spatial senses of vision, audition, and, to a lesser extent, touch. However, recent years have seen increasing interest in the nature of any crossmodal interactions involving the chemosensory modalities (i.e., smell and taste). Perhaps most relevant here has been interest in the use of olfactory cues while driving (e.g., to awaken/alert the drowsy driver). Some researchers have even contemplated the possibility of olfactory warning signals. However, one of the key problems is that the slower transduction of olfactory signals relative to stimuli from the other senses (see Spence & Squire, 2003), together with the fact that such cues would only likely be detected when a driver inhales in their respiratory cycle (that is, around every three to five seconds in the normal adult), means they are not well-suited to the delivery of time-critical warnings. What is more, the evidence that has been published to date also suggests that olfactory cues will likely not awaken the driver if they have actually fallen asleep (see Badia, Wesensten, Lammers, Culpepper, & Harsh, 1990; Carskadon & Herz, 2004). Rather, the interest of using olfactory stimuli would seem to be more in terms of increasing immersion in the driving scene, e.g., releasing the scent of pine when the satnav thinks that you are driving through the forest, say (see Ho & Spence, 2013, for a review).

A number of studies have, though, demonstrated that the periodic presentation of pulses of olfactory stimulation can facilitate participants' performance on a range of visual vigilance and compatibility tasks (see Ho & Spence, 2005a; Warm, Dember, & Parasuraman, 1991; see also Baron & Kalsher, 1998; Martin & Cooper, 2007). This kind of crossmodal alerting effect is likely to work via a spatially non-specific modulation of arousal. However, similar to what happens with images and their characteristic sounds (see Section 2.7), it is worth noting that more recent research has demonstrated that visual attention can be drawn to those stimuli that are associated with the presentation of their characteristic aroma/smell. So, for example, it has been reported that participants detect orange-coloured targets more rapidly when smelling an orange or citrus aroma, whereas the scent of strawberries will draw their attention towards (or prioritize) the red items in the scene instead (see Chen, Zhou, Chen, He, & Zhou, 2013; Seigneuric, Durand, Jiang, Baudouin, & Schaal, 2010; Seo, Roidl, Müller, & Negoias, 2010; see also Allen & Schwartz, 1940, for early research in this area). Note here that such crossmodal exogenous attentional effects would appear to be based both on specific object associations as well as on more abstract odour-colour associations. Putting such research findings in the driving context, one could perhaps imagine that the smell of petrol might prime the driver's awareness of other road vehicles. That said, such unpleasant traffic smells have also been associated with an increase in road rage incidents so, all in all, this would probably not be the best idea (Fumento, 1998).

Thus, while such crossmodal links in attention between the chemosensory and spatial modalities are undoubtedly interesting in their own right, it is, as yet, hard to see how they might be incorporated into the design of car interface/ warning signals. What is more, it should be noted that having to monitor, or else otherwise attend to, the olfactory channel has been shown to impair the speed of participants' responses to target stimuli presented in one of the spatial senses (see Marks & Wheeler, 1998; Spence, Kettenmann, Kobal, & McGlone, 2000, 2001a, 2001b). In other words, despite the relatively unique position of olfaction in terms of its limited access to neural resources (see Stevenson & Attuquayefilo, 2013), attentional mechanisms do appear to be linked between olfaction and the other senses (see Spence, 2019b, for a review). And, going in the opposite direction, see Forster and Spence (2018) for recent evidence that increasing visual load can induce a lack of olfactory awareness (see also Schreiber & White, 2013; van der Wal & Van Dillen, 2013). So, although not playing a central role as yet, crossmodal attention research that engages with the chemical senses may come to play a small but significant role in driving in the years ahead.

6 Conclusions

In this Element, we have thoroughly reviewed the burgeoning literature on crossmodal attention, both basic and applied, that has flourished over the last half century or so (see Spence, 2010a, 2010b, for earlier reviews). As we have seen at multiple points, the laboratory-based research has primarily tended to focus on trying to understand the cognitive neuroscience underpinnings of crossmodal links in attention between the spatial senses of vision, audition, and touch. In general, while our understanding of the neural mechanisms and structures underpinning the ability to direct attention spatially, as well as to a specific sensory modality, have undoubtedly come a long way, the laboratory research has tended to concentrate on a small number of experimental paradigms mostly involving the presentation of stimuli in a relatively constrained region of space directly in front of, and close to, the participant. The laboratory research can also be criticized, at least from an applied perspective, for its focus on meaningless stimuli, and for failing to pay much heed to the response dimension (i.e., most studies have simply used finger buttonpress responses).

Taken together, the extensive crossmodal constraints on the allocation of attention that have been identified by laboratory research conducted over the last half century have increasingly started to be incorporated into guidelines for the design of real-world interfaces and warning signals, especially in the context of driving. However, by setting crossmodal attention research in context, a number of important gaps between experimental studies and the potential problems arising from applied situations open further questions/unexplored avenues of research. Looking to the future, it will be interesting to probe further the way in which being in a moving vehicle while potentially aroused and/or at least at an elevated level of threat, as compared to the typical laboratory situation, changes crossmodal constraints on attentional selection in different regions of space (see Sambo & Iannetti, 2013; Van Damme, Crombez, & Spence, 2009). It will also be important to extend the findings collected primarily in neurologically healthy young adults to assess the situation faced by other groups of road users (e.g., older drivers) (see Hugenschmidt, Peiffer, McCoy, Hayasaka, & Laurienti, 2009; Poliakoff, Ashworth, Lowe, & Spence, 2006). Finally, here, while the focus in this Element has been squarely on the case of driving, given that this is where one finds that majority of the applied crossmodal attention research that has been published to date, it is important to note that a similar story has been emerging in a number of other application domains from the aircraft cockpit to the operating theatre and the trading floor (see Baldwin et al., 2012; Ngo et al., 2012; Oving, Veltmann, & Bronkhorst, 2004; Previc, 2000; Sarter, 2000; Stanney et al., 2004). As such, one can consider this Element in the context of Paul Rozin's (2006) call to arms for applied researchers to focus more on domain-based research rather than focusing solely on process-based (i.e., attention, perception, memory, cognition) research.

References

Abrams, R. A., Davoli, C. C., Du, F., Knapp, W. H., III, & Paull, D. (2008). Altered vision near the hands. *Cognition*, **107**, 1035–47.

Ahtamad, M., Gray, R., Ho, C., Reed, N., & Spence, C. (2015). Informative collision warnings: Effect of modality and driver age. In *Proceedings of the 8th International Driving Symposium on Human Factors in Driver Assessment, Training and Vehicle Design* (pp. 323–9). June, Salt Lake City, UT.

Ahveninen, J., Ingalls, G., Yildirim, F., Calabro, F. J., & Vaina, L. M. (2019). Peripheral visual localization is degraded by globally incongruent auditory-spatial attention cues. *Experimental Brain Research*, **237**, 2137–43.

Alais, D., & Burr, D. (2004). The ventriloquist effect results from near-optimal bimodal integration. *Current Biology*, **14**, 257–62.

Alais, D., Morrone, C., & Burr, D. (2006). Separate attentional resources for vision and audition. *Proceedings of the Royal Society B*, **273**, 1339–45.

Allen, F., & Schwartz, M. (1940). The effect of stimulation of the senses of vision, hearing, taste, and smell upon the sensibility of the organs of vision. *Journal of General Physiology*, **24**, 105–21.

Alsius, A., Möttönen, R., Sams, M. E., Soto-Faraco, S., & Tiippana, K. (2014). Effect of attentional load on audiovisual speech perception: Evidence from ERPs. *Frontiers in Psychology*, **5**, 727.

Alsius, A., Navarra, J., Campbell, R., & Soto-Faraco, S. (2005). Audiovisual integration of speech falters under high attention demands. *Current Biology*, **15**, 1–5.

Alsius, A., Navarra, J., & Soto-Faraco, S. (2007). Attention to touch weakens audiovisual speech integration. *Experimental Brain Research*, **183**, 399–404.

Amado, C., Kovács, P., Mayer, R., Ambrus, G. G., Trapp, S., & Kovács, G. (2018). Neuroimaging results suggest the role of prediction in cross-domain priming. *Scientific Reports*, **8**, 10356.

Amado, S., & Ulupinar, P. (2005). The effects of conversation on attention and peripheral detection: Is talking with a passenger and talking on the cell phone different? *Transportation Research Part F: Traffic Psychology and Behaviour*, **8**, 383–95.

Andersen, T. S., Tiippana, K., & Sams, M. (2004). Factors influencing audiovisual fission and fusion illusions. *Cognitive Brain Research*, **21**, 301–8.

Andersen, T. S., Tiippana, K., & Sams, M. (2005). Maximum likelihood integration of rapid flashes and beeps. *Neuroscience Letters*, **380**, 155–60.

Arnell, K. M. (2006). Visual, auditory, and cross-modality dual-task costs: Electrophysiological evidence for an amodal bottleneck on working memory consolidation. *Perception & Psychophysics*, **68**, 447–57.

Arnell, K. M., & Jenkins, R. (2004). Revisiting within modality and cross-modality attentional blinks: Effects of target-distractor similarity. *Perception & Psychophysics*, **66**, 1147–61.

Arnell, K. M., & Larson, J. M. (2002). Cross-modality attentional blink without preparatory task-set switching. *Psychonomic Bulletin & Review*, **9**, 497–506.

Arrighi, R., Lunardi, R., & Burr, D. (2011). Vision and audition do not share attentional resources in sustained tasks. *Frontiers in Psychology*, **2:56**, 1–4.

Ashley, S. (2001). Driving the info highway. *Scientific American*, **285**(4), 44–50.

Atmaca, S., Sebanz, N., & Knoblich, G. (2011). The joint flanker effect: Sharing tasks with real and imagined co-actors. *Experimental Brain Research*, **211**, 371–85. http://doi.org/10.1007/s00221-011-2709-9

Azañón, E., Camacho, K., & Soto-Faraco, S. (2010). Tactile remapping beyond space. *European Journal of Neuroscience*, **31**, 1858–67.

Azañón, E., & Soto-Faraco, S. (2008a). Changing reference frames during the encoding of tactile events. *Current Biology*, **18**, 1044–9.

Azañón, E., & Soto-Faraco, S. (2008b). Spatial remapping of tactile events: Assessing the effects of frequent posture changes. *Communicative & Integrative Biology*, **1**, 45–6.

Azañón, E., Stenner, M. P., Cardini, F., & Haggard, P. (2015). Dynamic tuning of tactile localization to body posture. *Current Biology*, **25**, 512–17.

Badde, S., Röder, B., & Heed, T. (2019). Feeling a touch to the hand on the foot. *Current Biology*, **29**, 1491–7.

Badia, P., Wesensten, N., Lammers, W., Culpepper, J., & Harsh, J. (1990). Responsiveness to olfactory stimuli presented in sleep. *Physiology & Behavior*, **48**, 87–90.

Baier, B., Kleinschmidt, A., & Müller, N. (2006). Cross-modal processing in early visual and auditory cortices depends on the statistical relation of multisensory information. *Journal of Neuroscience*, **26**, 12260–5.

Baldwin, C. L. (2011). Verbal collision avoidance messages during simulated driving: Perceived urgency, alerting effectiveness and annoyance. *Ergonomics*, **54**, 328–37.

Baldwin, C. L., Spence, C., Bliss, J. P., Brill, J. C., Wogalter, M. S., Mayhorn, C. B., & Ferris, T. K. (2012). Multimodal cueing: The relative benefits of the auditory, visual, and tactile channels in complex environments. *Proceedings of the 56th Human Factors and Ergonomics Society meeting*, **56**, 1431–5.

Baron, R. A., & Kalsher, M. J. (1998). Effects of a pleasant ambient fragrance on simulated driving performance: The sweet smell of . . . safety? *Environment and Behavior*, **30**, 535–52.

Battaglia, P. W., Jacobs, R. A., & Aslin, R. N. (2003). Bayesian integration of visual and auditory signals for spatial localization. *Journal of the Optical Society of America A*, **20**, 1391–7.

Battistoni, E., Kaiser, D., Hickey, C., & Peelen, M. V. (2018). Spatial attention follows category-based attention during naturalistic visual search: Evidence from MEG decoding. *BioRxiv*, 390807.

Bauer, M., Kennett, S., & Driver, J. (2012). Attentional selection of location and modality in vision and touch modulates low-frequency activity in associated sensory cortices. *Journal of Neurophysiology*, **107**, 2342–51.

Baumeister, R. F., Vohs, K. D., & Funder, D. C. (2007). Psychology as the science of self-reports and finger movements: Whatever happened to actual behavior? *Perspectives on Psychological Science*, **2**, 396–403.

Begault, D. R., & Pittman, M. T. (1996). Three-dimensional audio versus head-down traffic alert and collision avoidance system displays. *International Journal of Aviation Psychology*, **6**, 79–93.

Belz, S. M., Robinson, G. S., & Casali, J. G. (1999). A new class of auditory warning signals for complex systems: Auditory icons. *Human Factors*, **41**, 608–18.

Benoni, H., & Tsal, Y. (2010). Where have we gone wrong? Perceptual load does not affect selective attention. *Vision Research*, **50**, 1292–8.

Benoni, H., & Tsal, Y. (2013). Conceptual and methodological concerns in the theory of perceptual load. *Frontiers in Psychology*, **4**, 522. http://doi.org/10.3389/fpsyg.2013.00522

Berger, A., Henik, A., & Rafal, R. (2005). Competition between endogenous and exogenous orienting of visual attention. *Journal of Experimental Psychology: General*, **134**, 207–21. http://doi.org/10.1037/0096-3445.134.2.207

Berman, R. A., & Colby, C. L. (2002). Auditory and visual attention modulate motion processing in area MT+. *Cognitive Brain Research*, **14**, 64–74.

Bertelson, P., Vroomen, J., de Gelder, B., & Driver, J. (2000). The ventriloquist effect does not depend on the direction of deliberate visual attention. *Perception & Psychophysics*, **62**, 321–32.

Biondi, F., Leo, M., Gastaldi, M., Rossi, R., & Mulatti, C. (2016). How to drive drivers nuts: Effects of auditory, vibrotactile, and multimodal warnings on perceived urgency, annoyance and acceptability. Presentation at the *Transportation Research Board 96th Annual Meeting*, February.

Biondi, F., Strayer, D., Rossi, R., Gastaldi, M., & Mulatti, C. (2017). Advanced driver assistance systems: Using multimodal redundant warnings to enhance road safety. *Applied Ergonomics*, **58**, 238–44.

Blurton, S. P., Greenlee, M. W., & Gondan, M. (2015). Cross-modal cueing in audiovisual spatial attention. *Attention, Perception, & Psychophysics*, **77**, 2356–76.

Blustein, D., Gill, S., Wilson, A., & Sensinger, J. (2019). Crossmodal congruency effect scores decrease with repeat test exposure. *PeerJ*, **7**, e6976. http://doi.org/10.7717/peerj.6976

Bollimunta, A., Bogadhi, A. R., & Krauzlis, R. J. (2018). Comparing frontal eye field and superior colliculus contributions to covert spatial attention. *Nature Communications*, **9**, 3553. http://doi.org/10.1038/s41467-018-06042-2

Bolognini, N., Frassinetti, F., Serino, A., & Làdavas, E. (2005). 'Acoustical vision' of below threshold stimuli: Interaction among spatially converging audiovisual inputs. *Experimental Brain Research*, **160**, 273–82.

Brang, D., Towle, V. L., Suzuki, S., Hillyard, S. A., Di Tusa, S., Dai, Z., Tao, J., Wu, S., & Grabowecky, M. (2015). Peripheral sounds rapidly activate visual cortex: Evidence from electrocorticography. *Journal of Neurophysiology*, **114**, 3023–8. http://doi.org/10.1152/jn.00728.2015

Brewster, S., & Brown, L. M. (2004). Tactons: Structured tactile messages for non-visual information display. *Proceedings of the Fifth Australasian User Interface Conference (AUIC '04)*, pp. 15–24. Dunedin, New Zealand: Australian Computer Society. Conferences in Research and Practice in Information Technology, 28 (A. Cockburn, Ed.).

Briand, K. A., & Klein, R. M. (1987). Is Posner's 'beam' the same as Treisman's 'glue'?: On the relation between visual orienting and feature integration theory. *Journal of Experimental Psychology: Human Perception and Performance*, **13**, 228–41.

Brown, I. D. (2001). *A review of the 'looked but failed to see' accident causation factor*. Behavioural Research in Road Safety. Eleventh Seminar, UK. Department for Transport. https://webarchive.nationalarchives.gov.uk/20100209094331/http://www.dft.gov.uk/print/pgr/roadsafety/research/behavioural/archive/behaviouralresearchinroadsaf4682#a1169

Brozzoli, C., Cardinali, L., Pavani, F., & Farnè, A. (2010). Action-specific remapping of peripersonal space. *Neuropsychologia*, **48**, 796–802.

Brozzoli, C., Pavani, F., Cardinali, L., Urquizar, C., Cardinali, L., & Farnè, A. (2009). Grasping actions remap peripersonal space. *Neuroreport*, **20**, 913–17.

Buchtel, H. A., & Butter, C. M. (1988). Spatial attention shifts: Implications for the role of polysensory mechanisms. *Neuropsychologia*, **26**, 499–509.

Buschman, T. J., & Miller, E. K. (2007). Top-down versus bottom-up control of attention in the prefrontal and posterior parietal cortices. *Science*, **315**, 1860–2.

Busse, L., Roberts, K. C., Crist, R. E., Weissman, D. H., & Woldorff, M. G. (2005). The spread of attention across modalities and space in a multisensory object. *Proceedings of the National Academy of Sciences of the USA*, **102**, 18751–6.

Campus, C., Sandini, G., Morrone, M. C., & Gori, M. (2017). Spatial localization of sound elicits early responses from occipital visual cortex in humans. *Scientific Reports*, **7**, 10415.

Cappe, C., Thelen, A., Romei, V., Thut, G., & Murray, M. (2012). Looming signals reveal synergistic principles of multisensory integration. *Journal of Neuroscience*, **32**, 1171–82. http://doi.org/10.1523/JNEUROSCI.5517–11.2012

Carlander, O., Eriksson, L., & Oskarsson, P.-A. (2007). Handling uni- and multi-modal threat cuing with simultaneous radio calls in a combat vehicle setting. In C. Stephanidis (Ed.), *Proceedings of HCI International 2007* (HCI Part II, HCI 2007, LNCS 4555) (pp. 293–302). Berlin, Germany: Springer-Verlag.

Carrasco, M. (2011). Visual attention: The past 25 years. *Vision Research*, **51**: 1484–1525. http://doi.org/10.1016/j.visres.2011.04.012

Carskadon, M. A., & Herz, R. S. (2004). Minimal olfactory perception during sleep: Why odor alarms will not work for humans. *Sleep*, **27**, 402–5.

Castro, L., Soto-Faraco, S., Morís Fernández, L., & Ruzzoli, M. (2018). The breakdown of the Simon effect in cross-modal contexts: EEG evidence. *European Journal of Neuroscience*, **47**, 832–44.

Chambers, C. D., Payne, J. M., & Mattingley, J. B. (2007). Parietal disruption impairs reflexive spatial attention within and between sensory modalities. *Neuropsychologia*, **45**, 1715–24.

Chambers, C. D., Stokes, M. G., & Mattingley, J. B. (2004). Modality-specific control of strategic spatial attention in parietal cortex. *Neuron*, **44**, 925–30.

Chan, A., MacLean, K. E., & McGrenere, J. (2005). Learning and identifying haptic icons under workload. In *Proceedings of the 1st World Haptics Conference (WHC '05)*, Pisa, Italy, pp. 432–9.

Chan, A. H. S., & Chan, K. W. L. (2006). Synchronous and asynchronous presentations of auditory and visual signals: Implications for control console design. *Applied Ergonomics*, **37**, 131–40.

Chen, K., Zhou, B., Chen, S., He, S., & Zhou, W. (2013). Olfaction spontaneously highlights visual saliency map. *Proceedings of the Royal Society B. Biological Sciences*, **280**: 20131729.

Chen, X., Chen, Q. I., Gao, D., & Yue, Z. (2012). Interaction between endogenous and exogenous orienting in crossmodal attention. *Scandinavian Journal of Psychology*, **53**, 303–8.

Chen, Y.-C., & Spence, C. (2013). The time-course of the cross-modal semantic modulation of visual picture processing by naturalistic sounds and spoken words. *Multisensory Research*, **26**, 371–86.

Chen, Y.-C., & Spence, C. (2017). Hemispheric asymmetry: A novel signature of attention's role in multisensory integration. *Psychonomic Bulletin & Review*, **24**, 690–707.

Chica, A. B., Bartolomeo, P., & Lupiáñez, J. (2013). Two cognitive and neural systems for endogenous and exogenous spatial attention. *Behavioural Brain Research*, **237**, 107–23.

Chica, A., Sanabria, D., Lupiáñez, J., & Spence, C. (2007). Comparing intra-modal and crossmodal cuing in the endogenous orienting of spatial attention. *Experimental Brain Research*, **179**, 353–64, 531.

Chiou, R., & Rich, A. N. (2012). Cross-modality correspondence between pitch and spatial location modulates attentional orienting. *Perception*, **41**, 339–53.

Chun, M. M., Golomb, J. D., & Turk-Browne, N. B. (2011). A taxonomy of external and internal attention. *Annual Review of Psychology*, **62**, 73–101. http://doi.org/10.1146/annurev.psych.093008.100427

Ciaramitaro, V. M., Chow, H. M., & Eglington, L. G. (2017). Cross-modal attention influences auditory contrast sensitivity: Decreasing visual load improves auditory thresholds for amplitude- and frequency-modulated sounds. *Journal of Vision*, **17**, 20. http://doi.org/10.1167/17.3.20

Cléry, J., Guipponi, O., Odouard, S., Wardak, C., & Ben Hamed, S. (2015). Impact prediction by looming visual stimuli enhances tactile detection. *Journal of Neuroscience*, **35**, 4179–89.

Conrad, V., Kleiner, M., Bartels, A., Hartcher-O'Brien, J., Bülthoff, H. H., & Noppeney, U. (2013). Naturalistic stimulus structure determines the integration of audiovisual looming signals in binocular rivalry. *PLoS ONE*, **8**, e70710. http://doi.org/10.1371/journal.pone.0070710

Corbetta, M., & Shulman, G. L. (2002). Control of goal-directed and stimulus-driven attention in the brain. *Nature Reviews Neuroscience*, **3**, 201–15.

Dalton, P., Lavie, N., & Spence, C. (2009a). The role of working memory in tactile selective attention. *Quarterly Journal of Experimental Psychology*, **62**, 635–44.

Dalton, P., Santangelo, V., & Spence, C. (2009b). The role of working memory in auditory selective attention. *Quarterly Journal of Experimental Psychology*, **62**, 2126–32.

de Gelder, B., & Bertelson, P. (2003). Multisensory integration, perception and ecological validity. *Trends in Cognitive Sciences*, **7**, 460–7.

de Haan, B., Morgan, P. S., & Rorden, C. (2008). Covert orienting of attention and overt eye movements activate identical brain regions. *Brain Research*, **1204**, 102–11. http://doi.org/10.1016/j.brainres.2008.01.105

Deatherage, B. H. (1972). Auditory and other sensory forms of information processing. In H. P. Van Cott & R. G. Kinkade (Eds.), *Human engineering guide to equipment design* (pp. 124–60). New York, NY: John Wiley and Sons.

Dehais, F., Causse, M., Vachon, F., Régis, N., Menant, E., & Tremblay, S. (2014). Failure to detect critical auditory alerts in the cockpit: Evidence for inattentional deafness. *Human Factors*, 56, 631–644. http://doi.org/10.1177/0018720813510735

Dell'Acqua, R., Jolicoeur, P., Pesciarelli, F., Job, R., & Palomba, D. (2003). Electrophysiological evidence of visual encoding deficits in a cross-modal attentional blink paradigm. *Psychophysiology*, **40**, 629–39.

Dell'Acqua, R., Jolicoeur, P., Sessa, P., & Turatto, M. (2006). Attentional blink and selection in the tactile domain. *European Journal of Cognitive Psychology*, **18**, 537–59.

Dell'Acqua, R., Turatto, M., & Jolicoeur, P. (2001). Cross-modal attentional deficits in processing tactile stimulation. *Perception & Psychophysics*, **63**, 777–89.

De Meo, R., Murray, M. M., Clarke, S., & Matusz, P. J. (2015). Top-down control and early multisensory processes: Chicken vs. egg. *Frontiers in Integrative Neuroscience*, **9**, 17.

di Pellegrino, G., Làdavas, E., & Farné, A. (1997). Seeing where your hands are. *Nature*, **388**, 730.

Diederich, A., & Colonius, H. (2019). Multisensory integration and exogenous spatial attention: A time-window-of-integration analysis. *Journal of Cognitive Neuroscience*, **31**, 699–710.

Dittrich, K., Bossert, M. L., Rothe-Wulf, A., & Klauer, K. C. (2017). The joint flanker effect and the joint Simon effect: On the comparability of processes underlying joint compatibility effects. *Quarterly Journal of Experimental Psychology*, **70**, 1808–23. http://doi.org/10.1080/17470218.2016.1207690

Doruk, D., Chanes, L., Malavera, A., Merabet, L. B., Valero-Cabré, A., Fregni, F. (2018). Cross-modal cueing effects of visuospatial attention on conscious soma-tosensory perception. *Heliyon*, **4**, e00595. http://doi.org/10.1016/j.heliyon.2018.e00595

Driver, J. (1996). Enhancement of selective listening by illusory mislocation of speech sounds due to lip-reading. *Nature*, **381**, 66–8.

Driver, J. (2001). A selective review of selective attention research from the past century. *British Journal of Psychology*, **92**, 53–78.

Driver, J., & Spence, C. [J.] (1994). Spatial synergies between auditory and visual attention. In C. Umiltà & M. Moscovitch (Eds.), *Attention and performance XV: Conscious and nonconcious information processing* (pp. 311–331). Cambridge, MA: MIT Press.

Driver, J., & Spence, C. (1998). Attention and the crossmodal construction of space. *Trends in Cognitive Sciences*, **2**, 254–62.

Driver, J., & Spence, C. (2004). Crossmodal spatial attention: Evidence from human performance. In C. Spence & J. Driver (Eds.), *Crossmodal space and crossmodal attention* (pp. 179–220). Oxford, UK: Oxford University Press.

Dufour, A. (1999). Importance of attentional mechanisms in audiovisual links. *Experimental Brain Research*, **126**, 215–22.

Dufour, A., & Touzalin, P. (2008). Improved sensitivity in the perihand space. *Experimental Brain Research*, **190**, 91–8.

Duncan, J., Martens, S., & Ward, R. (1997). Restricted attentional capacity within but not between sensory modalities. *Nature*, **387**, 808–10.

Edworthy, J., & Hellier, E. (2006). Complex nonverbal auditory signals and speech warnings. In M. S. Wogalter (Ed.), *Handbook of warnings* (pp. 199–220). Mahwah, NJ: Lawrence Erlbaum.

Eimer, M. (1999). Can attention be directed to opposite directions in different modalities? An ERP study. *Clinical Neurophysiology*, **110**, 1252–9.

Eimer, M. (2004). Electrophysiology of human crossmodal spatial attention. In C. Spence & J. Driver (Eds.), *Crossmodal space and crossmodal attention* (pp. 221–45). Oxford, UK: Oxford University Press.

Eimer, M., Cockburn, D., Smedley, B., & Driver, J. (2001). Cross-modal links in endogenous spatial attention are mediated by common external locations: Evidence from event-related brain potentials. *Experimental Brain Research*, **139**, 398–411.

Eimer, M., & Driver, J. (2001). Crossmodal links in endogenous and exogenous spatial attention: Evidence from event-related brain potential studies. *Neuroscience and Biobehavioral Reviews*, **25**, 497–511.

Eimer, M., Van Velzen, J., & Driver, J. (2004). ERP evidence for cross-modal audiovisual effects of endogenous spatial attention within hemifields. *Journal of Cognitive Neuroscience*, **16**, 272–88.

Engel, A. K., Maye, A., Kurthen, M., & König, P. (2013). Where's the action? The pragmatic turn in cognitive science. *Trends in Cognitive Sciences*, **17**, 202–9. http://doi.org/10.1016/j.tics.2013.03.006

Eramudugolla, R., Kamke, M., Soto-Faraco, S., & Mattingley, J. B. (2011). Perceptual load influences auditory space perception in the ventriloquist aftereffect. *Cognition*, **118**, 62–74.

Ernst, M. O. (2012). Optimal multisensory integration: Assumptions and limits. In B. E. Stein (Ed.), *The new handbook of multisensory perception* (pp. 527–43). Cambridge, MA: MIT Press.

Ernst, M. O., & Banks, M. S. (2002). Humans integrate visual and haptic information in a statistically optimal fashion. Nature, 415(6870), 429–433.

Ernst, M. O., & Bülthoff, H. H. (2004). Merging the senses into a robust percept. *Trends in Cognitive Sciences*, **8**, 162–9.

Fairhall, S. L., & Macaluso, E. (2009). Spatial attention can modulate audio-visual integration at multiple cortical and subcortical sites. *European Journal of Neuroscience*, **29**, 1247–57.

Farah, M. J., Wong, A. B., Monheit, M. A., & Morrow, L. A. (1989). Parietal lobe mechanisms of spatial attention: Modality-specific or supramodal? *Neuropsychologia*, **27**, 461–70.

Farnè, A., Demattè, M. L., & Làdavas, E. (2003). Beyond the window: Multisensory representation of peripersonal space across a transparent barrier. *International Journal of Psychophysiology*, **50**, 51–61.

Farnè, A., & Làdavas, E. (2002). Auditory peripersonal space in humans. *Journal of Cognitive Neuroscience*, **14**, 1030–43.

Feng, W., Störmer, V. S., Martinez, A., McDonald, J. J., & Hillyard, S. A. (2014). Sounds activate visual cortex and improve visual discrimination, *Journal of Neuroscience*, **34**, 9817–24. http://doi.org/10.1523/JNEUROSCI.4869-13.2014

Feng, W., Störmer, V. S., Martinez, A., McDonald, J. J., & Hillyard, S. A. (2017). Involuntary orienting of attention to a sound desynchronizes the occipital alpha rhythm and improves visual perception. *Neuroimage*, **150**, 318–28. http://doi.org/10.1016/j.neuroimage.2017.02.033

Ferris, T. K., & Sarter, N. B. (2008). Cross-modal links among vision, audition, and touch in complex environments. *Human Factors*, **50**, 17–26.

Ferris, T. K., & Sarter, N. (2011). Continuously informing vibrotactile displays in support of attention management and multitasking in anesthesiology. *Human Factors*, **53**, 600–11.

Fiebelkorn, I. C., Foxe, J. J., Butler, J. S., & Molholm, S. (2011). Auditory facilitation of visual-target detection persists regardless of retinal eccentricity and despite wide audiovisual misalignments. *Experimental Brain Research*, **213**, 167–74.

Fiebelkorn, I. C., Foxe, J. J., & Molholm, S. (2010). Dual mechanisms for the cross-sensory spread of attention: How much do learned associations matter? *Cerebral Cortex*, **20**, 109–20.

Fiebelkorn, I. C., Foxe, J. J., & Molholm, S. (2012). Attention and multisensory feature integration. In B. E. Stein (Ed.), *The new handbook of multisensory processing* (pp. 383–94). Cambridge, MA: MIT Press.

Fitch, G. M., Kiefer, R. J., Hankey, J. M., & Kleiner, B. M. (2007). Toward developing an approach for alerting drivers to the direction of a crash threat. *Human Factors*, **49**, 710–20.

Fong, M. C. M., Hui, N. Y., Fung, E. S. W., Chu, P. C. K., & Wang, W. S. Y. (2018). Conflict monitoring in multi-sensory flanker tasks: Efiects of cross-modal distractors on the N2 component. *Neuroscience Letters*, **670**, 31–5.

Forster, S., & Spence, C. (2018). 'What smell?' Temporarily loading visual attention induces a prolonged loss of olfactory awareness. *Psychological Science*, **29**, 1642–52.

Fumento, M. (1998). 'Road rage' versus reality. *Atlantic Monthly*, **282**, 12–17.

Gallace, A., Soto-Faraco, S., Dalton, P., Kreukniet, B., & Spence, C. (2008). Response requirements modulate tactile spatial congruency effects. *Experimental Brain Research*, **191**, 171–86.

Gallace, A., & Spence, C. (2014). *In touch with the future: The sense of touch from cognitive neuroscience to virtual reality*. Oxford: Oxford University Press.

Galli, G., Noel, J.-P., Canzoneri, E., Blanke, O., & Serino, A. (2015). The wheelchair as a full-body tool extending the peripersonal space. *Frontiers in Psychology*, **6**, 639. http://doi.org/10.3389/fpsyg.2015.00639

Gaver, W. W. (1986). Auditory icons: Using sound in computer interfaces. *Human-Computer Interaction*, **2**, 167–77.

Geissler, L. R. (1909). The measurement of attention. *The American Journal of Psychology*, **20**, 473–529. http://doi.org/10.2307/1412972

Getz, L. M., & Kubovy, M. (2018). Questioning the automaticity of audiovisual correspondences. *Cognition*, **175**, 101–108.

Gibney, K. D., Aligbe, E., Eggleston, B. A., Nunes, S. R., Kerkhoff, W. G., Dean, C. L., & Kwakye, L. D. (2017). Visual distractors disrupt audiovisual integration regardless of stimulus complexity. *Frontiers of Integrative Neuroscience*, **11**, 1. http://doi.org/10.3389/fnint.2017.00001

Gibson, J. J., & Crooks, L. E. (1938). A theoretical field-analysis of automobile-driving. *American Journal of Psychology*, **51**, 453–71.

Gondan, M., Lange, K., Rösler, F., & Röder, B. (2004). The redundant target effect is affected by modality switch costs. *Psychonomic Bulletin and Review*, **11**, 307–13.

Graham, R. (1999). Use of auditory icons as emergency warnings: Evaluation within a vehicle collision avoidance application. *Ergonomics*, **42**, 1233–48.

Gray, R., Mohebbi, R., & Tan, H. Z. (2009). The spatial resolution of cross-modal attention: Implications for the design of multimodal interfaces. *ACM Transactions on Applied Perception*, **6**, 1–14.

Graziano, M. S. A., & Gross, C. G. (1995). The representation of extrapersonal space: A possible role for bimodal, visual-tactile neurons. In M. S. Gazzaniga (Ed.), The cognitive neurosciences (p. 1021–1034). The MIT Press.

Graziano, M. S. A., Gross, C. G., Taylor, C. S. R., & Moore, T. (2004). A system of multimodal areas in the primate brain. In C. Spence & J. Driver (Eds.), *Crossmodal space and crossmodal attention* (pp. 51–67). Oxford, UK: Oxford University Press.

Green, J. J., Doesburg, S. M., Ward, L. W., & McDonald, J. J. (2011). Electrical neuroimaging of voluntary audiospatial attention: Evidence for a supramodal attention control network. *Journal of Neuroscience*, **31**, 3560–4.

Green, J. J., Teder-Sälejärvi, W. A., & McDonald, J. J. (2005). Control mechanisms mediating shifts of attention in auditory and visual space: A spatio-temporal ERP analysis. *Experimental Brain Research*, **166**, 358–69.

Groh, J. M., & Sparks, D. L. (1996). Saccades to somatosensory targets: 1. Behavioral characteristics. *Journal of Neurophysiology*, **75**, 412–27.

Gross, C. G., & Graziano, M. S. A. (1995). Multiple representations of space in the brain. *The Neuroscientist*, **1**, 43–50.

Gruenefeld, U., Löchen, A., Brueck, Y., Boll, S., & Heuten, W. (2018). Where to look: Exploring peripheral cues for shifting attention to spatially distributed out-of-view objects. *Automotive UI'18*, September 23–25, 2018, Toronto, ON, Canada. http://doi.org/10.1145/3239060.3239080

Hairston, W. D., Hodges, D. A., Casanova, R., Hayasaka, S., Kraft, R., Maldjian, J. A., & Burdette, J. H. (2008). Closing the mind's eye: Deactivation of visual cortex related to auditory task difficulty. *Neuroreport*, **19**, 151–4.

Hancock, P. A., Lawson, B. D., Cholewiak, R., Elliott, L. R., van Erp, J. B. F., Mortimer, B. J. P., Rupert, A., & Redden, E. S. (2015). Tactile cuing to augment multisensory human–machine interaction. *Ergonomics in Design*, **23**, 2–9.

Hancock, P. A., Mercado, J. E., Merlo, J., & Van Erp, J. B F. (2013). Improving target detection in visual search through the augmenting multi-sensory cues. *Ergonomics*, **56**, 729–38.

Hancock, P. A., Oron-Gilad, T., & Szalma, J. L. (2007). Elaborations of the multiple-resource theory of attention. In A. F. Kramer, D. A. Wiegmann, & A. Kirlik (Eds.), *Attention: From theory to practice* (pp. 45–56). Oxford, UK: Oxford University Press.

Hari, R., & Jousmäki, V. (1996). Preference of personal to extrapersonal space in a visuomotor task. *Journal of Cognitive Neuroscience*, **8**, 305–7.

Harmening, W. M., Orlowski, J., Ben-Shahar, O., & Wagner, H. (2011). Overt attention toward oriented objects in free-viewing barn owls. *Proceedings of the National Academy of Sciences of the USA*, **108**, 8461–6. http://doi.org/10.1073/pnas.1101582108

Hartcher-O'Brien, J., Soto-Faraco, S., & Adam, R. (2017). A matter of bottom-up or top-down processes: The role of attention in multisensory integration. *Frontiers in Integrative Neuroscience*, **11**, 5.

Hasson, U., Malach, R., & Heeger, D. J. (2010). Reliability of cortical activity during natural stimulation. *Trends in Cognitive Sciences*, **14**, 40–8. http://doi.org/10.1016/J.TICS.2009.10.011

Hediger, H. (1955). *Studies of the psychology and behaviour of captive animals in zoos and circuses*. New York, NY: Criterion Books.

Heed, T., Habets, B., Sebanz, N., & Knoblich, G. (2010). Others' actions reduce crossmodal integration in peripersonal space. *Current Biology*, **20**, 1345–9.

Heffner, R. S., & Heffner, H. E. (1992a). Evolution of sound localization in mammals. In D. B. Webster, R. R. Fay, & A. N. Popper (Eds.), *The evolutionary biology of hearing* (pp. 691–715). New York, NY: Springer-Verlag.

Heffner, R. S., & Heffner, H. E. (1992b). Visual factors in sound localization in mammals. *Journal of Comparative Neurology*, **317**, 219–32.

Hein, G., Parr, A., & Duncan, J. (2006). Within-modality and cross-modality attentional blinks in a simple discrimination task. *Perception & Psychophysics*, **68**, 54–61.

Helbig, H. B., & Ernst, M. O. (2008). Visual-haptic cue weighting is independent of modality-specific attention. *Journal of Vision*, 8, 21, 1–16.

Hillstrom, A. P., Shapiro, K., & Spence, C. (2002). Attentional and perceptual limitations in processing sequentially presented vibrotactile targets. *Perception & Psychophysics*, **64**, 1068–82.

Hillyard, S. A., Simpson, G. V., Woods, D. L., Van Voorhis, S., & Münte, T. F. (1984). Event-related brain potentials and selective attention to different modalities. In F. Reinoso-Suarez & C. Ajmone-Marson (Eds.), *Cortical integration* (pp. 395–414). New York, NY: Raven Press.

Hillyard, S. A., Störmer, V. S., Feng, W., Martinez, A., & McDonald, J. J. (2016). Cross-modal orienting of visual attention, *Neuropsychologia*, **83**, 170–8.

Hirst, R. J., Cragg, L., & Allen, H. A. (2018). Vision dominates in adults but not children: A meta-analysis of the Colavita effect. *Neuroscience & Biobehavioural Reviews*, **94**, 286–301.

Ho, C., Hollingworth, C., Hollingworth, C., & Spence, C. (2015). *Assessing the potential benefits of novel front and back bike symbol lights to improve drivers' awareness of cyclists on road*. Unpublished manuscript.

Ho, C., Reed, N., & Spence, C. (2007). Multisensory in-car warning signals for collision avoidance. *Human Factors*, **49**, 1107–1114.

Ho, C., Santangelo, V., & Spence, C. (2009). Multisensory warning signals: When spatial correspondence matters. *Experimental Brain Research*, **195**, 261–72.

Ho, C., & Spence, C. (2005a). Olfactory facilitation of dual-task performance. *Neuroscience Letters*, **389**, 35–40.

Ho, C., & Spence, C. (2005b). Assessing the effectiveness of various auditory cues in capturing a driver's visual attention. *Journal of Experimental Psychology: Applied*, **11**, 157–74.

Ho, C., & Spence, C. (2006). Verbal interface design: Do verbal directional cues automatically orient visual spatial attention? *Computers in Human Behavior*, **22**, 733–48.

Ho, C., & Spence, C. (2007). Head orientation biases tactile localization. *Brain Research*, **1144C**, 136–41.

Ho, C., & Spence, C. (2008). *The multisensory driver: Implications for ergonomic car interface design*. Aldershot, HA: Ashgate Publishing.

Ho, C., & Spence, C. (2009). Using peripersonal warning signals to orient a driver's gaze. *Human Factors*, **51**, 539–56.

Ho, C., & Spence, C. (2013). Affective multisensory driver interface design. *International Journal of Vehicle Noise and Vibration* (Special Issue on *Human Emotional Responses to Sound and Vibration in Automobiles*), **9**, 61–74. http://doi.org/10.1504/IJVNV.2013.053817

Ho, C., & Spence, C. (2014). Effectively responding to tactile stimulation: Do homologous cue and effector locations really matter? *Acta Psychologia*, **151**, 32–9.

Ho, C., Spence, C., & Gray, R. (2013). Looming auditory and vibrotactile collision warnings for safe driving. *Proceedings of the 7th International Driving Symposium on Human Factors in Driver Assessment, Training, and Vehicle Design*, 551–7.

Ho, C., Spence, C., & Tan, H. Z. (2005). Warning signals go multisensory. *Proceedings of HCI International* 2005, **9**, Paper No. 2284, 1–10.

Ho, C., Tan, H. Z., & Spence, C. (2005). Using spatial vibrotactile cues to direct visual attention in driving scenes. *Transportation Research Part F*, **8**, 397–412.

Ho, C., Tan, H. Z., & Spence, C. (2006). The differential effect of vibrotactile and auditory cues on visual spatial attention. *Ergonomics*, **49**, 724–38.

Holmes, N. P., & Spence, C. (2005). Beyond the body schema: Visual, prosthetic, and technological contributions to bodily perception and awareness. In G. Knoblich, I. M. Thornton, M. Grosjean, & M. Shiffrar (Eds.), *Human body perception from the inside out* (pp. 15–64). Oxford, UK: Oxford University Press.

Hopkins, K., Kass, S. J., Blalock, L. D., & Brill, J. C. (2017). Effectiveness of auditory and tactile crossmodal cues in a dual-task visual and auditory scenario. *Ergonomics*, **60**, 692–700. http://doi.org/10.1080/00140139.2016.1198495

Horowitz, M. J., Duff, D. F., & Stratton, L. O. (1964). Body-buffer zone: Exploration of personal space. *Archive of General Psychiatry*, **11**, 651–6.

Horrey, W. J., & Wickens, C. D. (2006). Examining the impact of cell phone conversations on driving using meta-analytic techniques. *Human Factors*, **48**, 196–205.

Houghton, R. J., Macken, W. J., & Jones, D. M. (2003). Attentional modulation of the visual motion aftereffect has a central cognitive locus: Evidence of interference by the postcategorical on the precategorical. *Journal of Experimental Psychology: Human Perception & Performance*, **29**, 731–40.

Hugenschmidt, C. E., Peiffer, A. M., McCoy, T. P., Hayasaka, S., & Laurienti, P. J. (2009). Preservation of crossmodal selective attention in healthy aging. *Experimental Brain Research*, **198**, 273–85.

Hyde, P. S., & Knudsen, E. I. (2002). The optic tectum controls visually guided adaptive plasticity in the owl's auditory space map. *Nature*, **415**, 73–6.

Hylan, J. P. (1903). The distribution of attention - I. *Psychological Review*, **10**, 373–403.

Ignashchenkova, A., Dicke, P. W., Haarmeier, T., & Their, P. (2004). Neuron-specific contribution of the superior colliculus to overt and covert shifts of attention. *Nature Neuroscience*, **7**, 56–64.

Iordanescu, L., Grabowecky, M., Franconeri, S., Theeuwes, J., & Suzuki, S. (2010). Characteristic sounds make you look at target objects more quickly. *Attention, Perception, and Psychophysics*, **72**, 1736–41.

Iordanescu, L., Grabowecky, M., & Suzuki, S. (2011). Object-based auditory facilitation of visual search for pictures and words with frequent and rare targets *Acta Psychologica*, **137**, 252–9. http://doi.org/10.1016/j.actpsy.2010.07.017

Iordanescu, L., Guzman-Martinez, E., Grabowecky, M., & Suzuki, S. (2008). Characteristic sound facilitates visual search. *Psychonomic Bulletin & Review*, **15**, 548–54.

Jack, B. N., O'Shea, R. P., Cottrell, D., & Ritter, W. (2013). Does the ventriloquist illusion assist selective listening? *Journal of Experimental Psychology: Human Perception & Performance*, **39**, 1496–502.

Jacoby, O., Hall, S. E., & Mattingley, J. B. (2012). A crossmodal crossover: Opposite effects of visual and auditory perceptual load on steady-state evoked potentials to irrelevant visual stimuli. *Neuroimage*, **61**, 1050–8.

James, W. (1890). *The principles of psychology* (2 Vols.). New York, NY: Henry Holt.

Jensen, A., Merz, S., Spence, C., & Frings, C. (2019). Overt spatial attention modulates multisensory selection. *Journal of Experimental Psychology: Human Perception & Performance*, **45**, 174–88.

Jensen, A., Merz, S., Spence, C., & Frings, C. (2020). Interference of irrelevant information in multisensory selection depends on attentional set. *Attention, Perception, & Psychophysics*, 82, 1176–1195. http://doi.org/10.3758/s13414-019-01848-8

Johnen, A., Wagner, H., & Gaese, B. H. (2001). Spatial attention modulates sound localization in barn owls. *Journal of Physiology*, **85**, 1009–12.

Johnson, J. A., Strafella, A. P., & Zatorre, R. J. (2007). The role of the dorsolateral prefrontal cortex in bimodal divided attention: Two transcranial magnetic stimulation studies. *Journal of Cognitive Neuroscience*, **19**, 907–20.

Johnson, J. A., & Zatorre, R. J. (2006). Neural substrates for dividing and focusing attention between simultaneous auditory and visual events. *Neuroimage*, **31**, 1673–81.

Jolicoeur, P. (1999). Restricted attentional capacity between sensory modalities. *Psychonomic Bulletin & Review*, **6**, 87–92.

Jonides, J. (1981). Voluntary versus automatic control over the mind's eye's movement. In J. Long & A. Baddeley (Eds.), *Attention and performance* (Vol. 9, pp. 187–203). Hillsdale, NJ: Erlbaum.

Juan, C., Cappe, C., Alric, B., Roby, B., Gilardeau, S., Barone, P., & Girard, P. (2017). The variability of multisensory processes of natural stimuli in human and non-human primates in a detection task. *PLoS ONE*, **12**, e0172480.

Julesz, B., & Hirsh, I. J. (1972). Visual and auditory perception – An essay of comparison. In E. E. David Jr. & P. B. Denes (Eds.), *Human communication: A unified view* (pp. 283–340). New York, NY: McGraw-Hill.

Juravle, G., Binstead, G., & Spence, C. (2017). Tactile suppression in goal-directed movement. *Psychonomic Bulletin & Review*, **24**, 1060–76.

Just, M. A., Kellar, T. A., & Cynkar, J. (2008). A decrease in brain activation associated with driving when listening to someone speak. *Brain Research*, **1205**, 70–80.

Kahneman, D., & Treisman, A. (1984). Changing views of attention and automaticity. In R. Parasuraman & D. R. Davies (Eds.), *Varieties of attention* (pp. 26–61). San Diego, CA: Academic Press.

Kasper, R. W., Cecotti, H., Touryan, J., Eckstein, M. P., & Giesbrecht, B. (2014). Isolating the neural mechanisms of interference during continuous multisensory dual-task performance. *Journal of Cognitive Neuroscience*, **26**, 476–89.

Kawashima, R., O'Sullivan, B. T., & Roland, P. E. (1995). Positron-emission tomography studies of cross-modality inhibition in selective attentional tasks: Closing the 'mind's eye'. *Proceedings of the National Academy of Science, USA*, **92**, 5969–72.

Keil, A., Bradley, M. M., Junghöfer, M., Russmann, T., Lowenthal, W., & Lang, P. J. (2007). Cross-modal attention capture by affective stimuli: Evidence from event-related potentials. *Cognitive, Affective, & Behavioral Neuroscience*, **7**, 18–24.

Keil, J., Pomper, U., & Senkowski, D. (2016). Distinct patterns of local oscillatory activity and functional connectivity underlie intersensory attention and temporal prediction. *Cortex*, **74**, 277–88. http://doi.org/10.1016/j.cortex.2015.10.023

Kennett, S., Eimer, M., Spence, C., & Driver, J. (2001). Tactile-visual links in exogenous spatial attention under different postures: Convergent evidence from psychophysics and ERPs. *Journal of Cognitive Neuroscience*, **13**, 462–78.

Kennett, S., Spence, C., & Driver, J. (2002). Visuo-tactile links in covert exogenous spatial attention remap across changes in unseen hand posture. *Perception & Psychophysics*, **64**, 1083–94.

Kida, T., Inui, K., Wasaka, T., Akatsuka, K., Tanaka, E., & Kakigi, R. (2007). Time-varying cortical activations related to visual-tactile cross-modal links in spatial selective attention. *Journal of Neurophysiology*, **97**, 3585–96.

Kitagawa, N., & Spence, C. (2005). Investigating the effect of a transparent barrier on the crossmodal congruency effect. *Experimental Brain Research*, **161**, 62–71.

Kitagawa, N., Zampini, M., & Spence, C. (2005). Audiotactile interactions in near and far space. *Experimental Brain Research*, **166**, 528–37.

Klapetek, A., Ngo, M. K., & Spence, C. (2012). Do crossmodal correspondences enhance the facilitatory effect of auditory cues on visual search? *Attention, Perception, & Psychophysics*, **74**, 1154–67.

Klein, R. (2000). Inhibition of return. *Trends in Cognitive Sciences*, **4**, 138–47.

Klein, R. M., Brennan, M., & Gilani, A. (1987, November). *Covert cross-modality orienting of attention in space*. Paper presented at the annual meeting of the Psychonomics Society, Seattle.

Knoeferle, K., Knoeferle, P., Velasco, C., & Spence, C. (2016). Multisensory brand search: How the meaning of sounds guides consumers' visual attention. *Journal of Experimental Psychology: Applied*, **22**, 196–210.

Knudsen, E. I. (1982). Auditory and visual maps of space in the optic tectum of the owl. *Journal of Neuroscience*, **2**, 1177–94.

Kóbor, I., Füredi, L., Kovács, G., Spence, C., & Vidnyánszky, Z. (2006). Back-to-front: Improved tactile discrimination performance in the space you can't see. *Neuroscience Letters*, **400**, 163–7.

Koelewijn, T., Bronkhorst, A., & Theeuwes, J. (2009a). Competition between auditory and visual spatial cues during visual task performance. *Experimental Brain Research*, **195**, 593–602.

Koelewijn, T., Bronkhorst, A., & Theeuwes, J. (2009b). Auditory and visual capture during focused visual attention. *Journal of Experimental Psychology: Human Perception & Performance*, **35**, 1303–15.

Koelewijn, T., Bronkhorst, A., & Theeuwes, J. (2010). Attention and the multiple stages of multisensory integration: A review of audiovisual studies. *Acta Psychologica*, **134**, 372–84.

Koster, E. H., Crombez, G., Van Damme, S., Verschuere, B., & De Houwer, J. (2004). Does imminent threat capture or hold attention? *Emotion*, **4**, 312–17.

Kreutzfeldt, M., Stephan, D. N., Sturm, W., Willems, K., & Koch, I. (2015). The role of crossmodal competition and dimensional overlap in crossmodal attention switching. *Acta Psychologica*, **155**, 67–76.

Kunar, M. A., Carter, R., Cohen, M., & Horowitz, T. S. (2008). Telephone conversation impairs sustained visual attention via a central bottleneck. *Psychonomic Bulletin & Review*, **15**, 1135–40.

Kustov, A. A., & Robinson, D. L. (1996). Shared neural control of attentional shifts and eye movements. *Nature*, **384**, 74–7.

Kvasova, D., Garcia-Vernet, L., & Soto-Faraco, S. (2019). Characteristic sounds facilitate object search in real-life scenes. *BioRxiv*, 563080.

Laeng, B., Brennen, T., Johannessen, K., Holmen, K., & Elvestad, R. (2002). Multiple reference frames in neglect? An investigation of the object-centred frame and the dissociation between 'near' and 'far' from the body by use of a mirror. *Cortex*, **38**, 511–28.

Lakatos, P., Chen, C. M., O'Connell, M. N., Mills, A., & Schroeder, C. E. (2007). Neuronal oscillations and multisensory interaction in primary auditory cortex. *Neuron*, **53**, 279–92.

Lange, K., & Röder, B. (2006). Orienting attention to points in time improves stimulus processing both within and across modalities. *Journal of Cognitive Neuroscience*, **18**, 715–29.

Lavie, N. (1995). Perceptual load as a necessary condition for selective attention. *Journal of Experimental Psychology: Human Perception & Performance*, **21**, 451–68.

Lavie, N. (2005). Distracted and confused? Selective attention under load. *Trends in Cognitive Sciences*, **9**, 75–82.

Lavie, N. (2010). Attention, distraction, and cognitive control under load. *Current Directions in Psychological Science*, **19**, 143–8.

Lee, J., & Spence, C. (2015). Audiovisual crossmodal cuing effects in front and rear space. *Frontiers in Psychology: Cognitive Science*, **6**, 1086.

Lee, J., & Spence, C. (2017). On the spatial specificity of audiovisual cross-modal exogenous cuing effects. *Acta Psychologica*, **177**, 78–88.

Lee, J., & Spence, C. (2018). Assessing the influence of sound parameters on crossmodal cuing in different regions of space. *Acta Psychologica*, **185**, 96–103.

Lee, J. D., Hoffman, J. D., & Hayes, E. (2004). Collision warning design to mitigate driver distraction. *CHI 2004* (24–29 April, Vienna), **6**, 65–72.

Lennie, P. (2003). The cost of cortical computation. *Current Biology*, **13**, 493–7.

Leo, F., Romei, V., Freeman, E., Ladavas, E., & Driver, J. (2011). Looming sounds enhance orientation sensitivity for visual stimuli on the same side as such sounds. *Experimental Brain Research*, **213**, 193–201.

Leone, L. M., & McCourt, M. E. (2013). The role of physical and physiological simultaneity in audiovisual multisensory facilitation. *i-Perception*, **4**, 213–28.

Levy, J., Pashler, H., & Boer, E. (2006). Central interference in driving: Is there any stopping the psychological refractory period? *Psychological Science*, **17**, 228–35.

Li, C., Chen, K., Han, H., Chui, D., & Wu, J. (2012). An fMRI study of the neural systems involved in visually cued auditory top-down spatial and temporal attention. *PLoS ONE*, **7**, e49948.

Lin, C. Y., & Hsu, C. C. (2010). Measurement of auditory cues in drivers' distraction. *Perceptual and Motor Skills*, **111**, 503–16.

Lloyd, D. M., Merat, N., McGlone, F., & Spence, C. (2003a). Crossmodal links between audition and touch in covert endogenous spatial attention. *Perception & Psychophysics*, **65**, 901–24.

Lloyd, D. M., Shore, D. I., Spence, C., & Calvert, G. A. (2003b). Multisensory representation of limb position in human premotor cortex. *Nature Neuroscience*, **6**, 17–18.

Lovejoy, L. P., & Krauzlis, R. J. (2010). Inactivation of primate superior colliculus impairs covert selection of signals for perceptual judgments. *Nature Neuroscience*, **13**, 261–6.

Lu, S. A., Wickens, C. D., Prinet, J. C., Hutchins, S. D., Sarter, N., & Sebok. A. (2013). Supporting interruption management and multimodal interface design: Three meta-analyses of task performance as a function of interrupting task modality. *Human Factors*, **55**, 697–724.

Lu, S., Wickens, C., Sarter, N., & Sebok, A. (2011). Informing the design of multimodal displays: A meta-analysis of empirical studies comparing auditory and tactile interruptions. In *Proceedings of the 55th Annual Meeting of the Human Factors and Ergonomics Society (HFES)*. Las Vegas, NV, September (pp. 142–4).

Lu, Z.-L., & Dosher, B. A. (1998). External noise distinguishes attention mechanisms. *Vision Research*, **38**, 1183–98.

Lu, Z.-L., & Dosher, B. A. (2000). Spatial attention: Different mechanisms for central and peripheral temporal precues? *Journal of Experimental Psychology: Human Perception and Performance*, **26**, 1534–48.

Lu, Z.-L., Tse, H. C., Dosher, B. A., Lesmes, L. A., Posner, C., & Chu, W. (2009). Intra- and crossmodal cuing of spatial attention: Time courses and mechanisms. *Vision Research*, **49**, 1081–96.

Lucas, P. A. (1995). An evaluation of the communicative ability of auditory icons and earcons. In G. Kramer, (Ed.), *Proceedings of the 2nd International Conference on Auditory Display ICAD '94* (pp. 121–8). Sante Fe: ICAD.

Lukas, S., Philipp, A. M., & Koch, I. (2010). Switching attention between modalities: Further evidence for visual dominance. *Psychological Research*, **74**, 255–67.

Lukas, S., Philipp, A. M., & Koch, I. (2014). Crossmodal attention switching: Auditory dominance in temporal discrimination tasks. *Acta Psychologica*, **153**, 139–46.

Lunn, J., Sjoblom, A., Ward, J., Soto-Faraco, S., & Forster, S. (2019). Multisensory enhancement of attention depends on whether you are already paying attention. *Cognition*, **187**, 38–49.

Lupiáñez, J., Milán, E. G., Tornay, F. J., Madrid, E., & Tudela, P. (1998). Does IOR occur in discrimination tasks?: Yes, it does, but later. *Perception & Psychophysics*, **59**, 1241–54.

Macaluso, E., Frith, C. D., & Driver, J. (2000). Modulation of human visual cortex by crossmodal spatial attention. *Science*, **289**, 1206–8.

Macaluso, E., Frith, C. D., & Driver, J. (2002a). Directing attention to locations and to sensory modalities: Multiple levels of selective processing revealed with PET. *Cerebral Cortex*, **12**, 357–68.

Macaluso, E., Frith, C. D., & Driver, J. (2002b). Supramodal effects of covert spatial orienting triggered by visual or tactile events. *Journal of Cognitive Neuroscience*, **14**, 389–401.

Macaluso, E., Noppeney, U., Talsma, D., Vercillo, T., Hartcher-O'Brien, J., & Adam, R. (2016). The curious incident of attention in multisensory integration: Bottom-up *vs.* top-down. *Multisensory Research*, **29**, 557–83.

MacDonald, J. S. P., & Lavie, N. (2011). Visual perceptual load induces inattentional deafness. *Attention, Perception, & Psychophysics*, **73**, 1780–9.

Mack, A., & Rock, I. (1998). *Inattentional blindness*. Cambridge, MA: MIT Press.

Maddox, R. K., Pospisil, D. A., Stecker, G. C., & Lee, A. K. (2014). Directing eye gaze enhances auditory spatial cue discrimination. *Current Biology*, **24**, 748–52. http://doi.org/10.1016/j.cub.2014.02.021

Maguire, E. A. (2012). Studying the freely-behaving brain with fMRI. *NeuroImage*, **62**, 1170–6.

Marks, L. E., & Wheeler, M. E. (1998). Attention and the detectability of weak taste stimuli. *Chemical Senses*, **23**, 19–29.

Martin, G. N., & Cooper, J. A. (2007). *Odour effects on simulated driving performance: Adding zest to difficult journeys*. Poster presented at the British Psychology Society Annual Conference. York, 21–23 March.

Mast, F., Frings, C., & Spence, C. (2017). Crossmodal attentional control sets between vision and audition. *Acta Psychologica*, **178**, 41–7.

Matusz, P. J., & Eimer, M. (2011). Multisensory enhancement of attentional capture in visual search. *Psychonomic Bulletin & Review*, **18**, 904–9.

Matusz, P. J., & Eimer, M. (2013). Top-down control of audiovisual search by bimodal search templates. *Psychophysiology*, **50**, 996–1009.

Matusz, P. J., Retsa, C., & Murray, M. M. (2016). The context-contingent nature of cross-modal activations of the visual cortex. *Neuroimage*, **125**, 996–1004. http://doi.org/10.1016/j.neuroimage.2015.11.016

Mazza, V., Turatto, M., Rossi, M., & Umiltà, C. (2007). How automatic are audiovisual links in exogenous spatial attention? *Neuropsychologia*, **45**, 514–22.

McDonald, J. J., Green, J. J., Störmer, V. S., & Hillyard, S. A. (2012). Crossmodal spatial cueing of attention influences visual perception. In M. M. Murray & M. T. Wallace (Eds.), *The neural bases of multisensory processes* (pp. 509–28). Boca Raton, FL: CRC Press.

McDonald, J. J., Störmer, V. S., Martinez, A., Feng, W., & Hillyard, S. A. (2013) Salient sounds activate human visual cortex automatically. *Journal of Neuroscience*, **33**, 9194–201. http://doi.org/10.1523/JNEUROSCI.5902-12.2013

McDonald, J. J., Teder-Sälejärvi, W. A., & Hillyard, S. A. (2000). Involuntary orienting to sound improves visual perception. *Nature*, **407**, 906–8.

McDonald, J. J., Teder-Sälejärvi, W. A., Di Russo, F., & Hillyard, S. A. (2005). Neural basis of auditory-induced shifts in visual time-order perception. *Nature Neuroscience*, **8**, 1197–202.

McDonald, J. J., Teder-Sälejärvi, W. A., & Ward, L. M. (2001). Multisensory integration and crossmodal attention effects in the human brain. *Science*, **292**, 1791.

McDonald, J. J., Whitman, C. J., Störmer, V. S., & Hillyard, S. A. (2014). Involuntary cross-modal spatial attention influences visual perception. In G. R. Mangun (Ed.), *Cognitive electrophysiology: Attention, signals mind* (pp. 82–94). New York, NY: Elsevier.

McEvoy, S. P., Stevenson, M. R., & Woodward, M. (2007a). The prevalence of, and factors associated with, serious crashes involving a distracting activity. *Accident Analysis & Prevention*, **39**, 475–82.

McEvoy, S. P., Stevenson, M. R., & Woodward, M. (2007b). The contribution of passengers versus mobile phone use to motor vehicle crashes resulting in hospital attendance by the driver. *Accident Analysis & Prevention*, **39**, 1170–6.

McKeown, J. D., & Isherwood, S. (2007). Mapping the urgency and pleasant-ness of speech, auditory icons, and abstract alarms to their referents within the vehicle. *Human Factors*, **49**, 417–28.

Meng, F., Ho, C., Gray, R., & Spence. C. (2015a). Dynamic vibrotactile signals for forward collision avoidance warning systems. *Human Factors*, **57**, 329–46.

Meng, F., Ho, C., Gray, R., & Spence. C. (2015b). Dynamic vibrotactile signals for forward collision avoidance: Toward the torso vs. toward the head. *Ergonomics*, **58**, 411–25.

Meng, F., & Spence, C. (2015). Tactile warning signals for collision avoidance. *Accident Analysis & Prevention*, **75**, 333–46.

Mercier, M. R., Foxe, J. J., Fiebelkorn, I. C., Butler, J. S., Schwartz, T. H., & Molholm, S. (2013). Auditory-driven phase reset in visual cortex: Human electrocorticography reveals mechanisms of early multisensory integration. *Neuroimage*, **79**, 19–29.

Merlo, J. L., Duley, A. R., & Hancock. P. A. (2010). Cross-modal congruency benefits for combined tactile and visual signaling. *American Journal of Psychology*, **123**, 413–24.

Merlo, J., & Hancock, P. (2011). Quantification of tactile cueing for enhanced target search capacity. *Military Psychology*, **23**, 137–53.

Michael, G. A., Dupuy, M.-A., Deleuze, A., Humblot, M., Simon, B., & Naveteur, J. (2012). Interacting effects of vision and attention in perceiving spontaneous sensations arising on the hands. *Experimental Brain Research*, **216**, 21–34.

Miles, E., Brown, R., & Poliakoff, E. (2011). Investigating the nature and time-course of the modality shift effect between vision and touch. *Quarterly Journal of Experimental Psychology*, **64**, 871–88.

Miller, J. O. (1982). Divided attention: Evidence for coactivation with redun-dant signals. *Cognitive Psychology*, **14**, 247–79.

Miller, J. O. (1991). Channel interaction and the redundant targets effect in bimodal divided attention. *Journal of Experimental Psychology: Human Perception and Performance*, **17**, 160–9.

Miller, J., Ulrich, R., & Rolke, B. (2009). On the optimality of serial and parallel processing in the psychological refractory period paradigm: Effects of the distribution of stimulus onset asynchronies. *Cognitive Psychology*, **58**, 273–310.

Moeller, B., Zoppke, H., & Frings, C. (2016). What a car does to your perception: Distance evaluations differ from within and outside of a car. *Psychonomic Bulletin & Review*, **23**, 781–8.

Mohebbi, R., Gray, R., & Tan, H. Z. (2009). Driver reaction time to tactile and auditory rear-end collision warnings while talking on a cell phone. *Human Factors*, **51**, 102–10.

Molloy, K, Griffiths, T. D., Chait, M., & Lavie, N. (2015). Inattentional deafness: Visual load leads to time-specific suppression of auditory evoked responses. *Journal of Neuroscience*, **35**, 16046–54. http://doi.org/10.1523/JNEUROSCI.2931-15.2015

Mondor, T. A., & Amirault, K. J. (1998). Effect of same- and different-modality spatial cues on auditory and visual target identification. *Journal of Experimental Psychology: Human Perception & Performance*, **24**, 745–55.

Mondor, T. A., & Zatorre, R. J. (1995). Shifting and focusing auditory spatial attention. *Journal of Experimental Psychology: Human Perception and Performance*, **21**, 387–409.

Montagne, C., & Zhou, Y. (2018). Audiovisual interactions in front and rear space. *Frontiers in Psychology*, **9**, 713. http://doi.org/10.3389/fpsyg.2018.00713

Moore, T., Armstrong, K. M., & Fallah, M. (2003). Visuomotor origins of covert spatial attention. *Neuron*, **40**, 671–83.

Moris-Fernández, L., Visser, M., Ventura-Campos, N., Ávila, C., & Soto-Faraco, S. (2015). Top-down attention regulates the neural expression of audiovisual integration. *NeuroImage*, **119**, 272–85.

Morrell, F. (1972). Visual system's view of acoustic space. *Nature*, **238**, 44–6.

Morrell, F. (1973). A reply to 'Comments on "Visual system's view of acoustic space" by Pöppel'. *Nature*, **243**, 231.

Moseley, G. L., Gallace, A., & Spence, C. (2012). Bodily illusions in health and disease: Physiological and clinical perspectives and the concept of a cortical 'body matrix'. *Neuroscience & Biobehavioural Reviews*, **36**, 34–46.

Mozolic, J. L., Joyner, D., Hugenschmidt, C. E., Peiffer, A. M., Kraft, R. A., Maldjian, J. A., & Laurienti, P. J. (2008). Cross-modal deactivations during modality-specific selective attention. *BMC Neurology*, **8**, 35.

Mueller, H. J., & Rabbitt, P. M. (1989). Reflexive and voluntary orienting of visual attention: Time course of activation and resistance to interruption. *Journal of Experimental Psychology: Human Perception and Performance*, **15**, 315–30. http://doi.org/10.1037/0096-1523.15.2.315

Mühlberg, S., Oriolo, G., & Soto-Faraco, S. (2014). Cross-modal decoupling in temporal attention. *European Journal of Neuroscience*, **39**, 2089–97.

Mühlberg, S., & Soto-Faraco, S. (2018). Cross-modal decoupling in temporal attention between audition and touch. *Psychological Research*, **83**, 1626–39. http://doi.org/10.1007/s00426-018-1023-6

Murphy, G., & Greene, C. M. (2017). Load theory behind the wheel; perceptual and cognitive load effects. *Canadian Journal of Experimental Psychology*, **71**, 191–202.

Murphy, S., & Dalton, P. (2016). Out of touch? Visual load induces inattentional numbness. *Journal of Experimental Psychology: Human Perception and Performance*, **42**, 761–5.

Murphy, S., Dalton, P., & Spence, C. (2017). Selective attention in vision, audition, and touch. In R. Menzel (Ed.), *Learning theory and behavior, Vol. 1 of Learning and memory: A comprehensive reference*, 2nd ed., J. Byrne (Series Ed.) (pp. 155–70). Oxford, UK: Academic Press.

Murphy, S., Spence, C., & Dalton, P. (2017). Auditory perceptual load: A critical review. *Hearing Research*, **352**, 40–8.

Nagel, S. K., Carl, C., Kringe, T., Märtin, R., & König, P. (2005). Beyond sensory substitution-learning the sixth sense. *Journal of Neural Engineering*, **2**, R13–R26.

Navarra, J., Alsius, A., Soto-Faraco, S., & Spence, C. (2009). Assessing the role of attention in the audiovisual integration of speech. *Information Fusion*, **11**, 4–11.

Naveteur, J., Honore, J., & Michael, G. A. (2005). How to detect an electrocutaneous shock which was not delivered? Overt spatial attention influences decision. *Behavioural Brain Research*, **165**, 254–61.

Ngo, M. K., Pierce, R., & Spence, C. (2012). Utilizing multisensory cues to facilitate air traffic management. *Human Factors*, **54**, 1093–103.

Nicholls, M. E. R., Roden, S., Thomas, N. A., Loetscher, T., Spence, C., & Forte, J. (2014). Close to me: The effect of asymmetrical environments on spatial attention. *Ergonomics*, **57**, 876–85.

Noel, J.-P., Grivaz, P., Marmaroli, P., Lissek, H., Blanke, O., & Serino, A. (2015). Full body action remapping of peripersonal space: The case of walking. *Neuropsychologia*, **70**, 375–84.

Noel, J.-P., Lukowska, M., Wallace, M., & Serino, A. (2016) Multisensory simultaneity judgment and proximity to the body. *Journal of Vision*, **16**, 21. http://doi.org/10.1167/16.3.21

Noel, J.-P., Modi, K., Wallace, M. T., & Van der Stoep, N. (2018). Audiovisual integration in depth: Multisensory binding and gain as a function of distance. *Experimental Brain Research*, **236**, 1939–51.

Nuku, P. & Bekkering, H. (2010). When one sees what the other hears: Crossmodal attentional modulation for gazed and non-gazed upon auditory targets. *Consciousness and Cognition*, **19**, 135–43.

Occelli, V., Hartcher-O'Brien, J., Spence, C., & Zampini, M. (2010). Assessing the audiotactile Colavita effect in near and rear space. *Experimental Brain Research*, **203**, 517–32.

Occelli, V., Spence, C., & Zampini, M. (2011). Audiotactile interactions in front and rear space. *Neuroscience & Biobehavioral Reviews*, **35**, 589–98.

Odegaard, B., Wozny, D. R., & Shams, L. (2016). The effects of selective and divided attention on sensory precision and integration. *Neuroscience Letters*, **614**, 24–8.

Ora, H., Wada, M., Salat, D., & Kansaku, K. (2016). Arm crossing updates brain functional connectivity of the left posterior parietal cortex. *Scientific Reports*, 6:28105. http://doi.org/10.1038/srep28105.

Oray, S., Lu, Z. L., & Dawson, M. E. (2002). Modification of sudden onset auditory ERP by involuntary attention to visual stimuli. *International Journal of Psychophysiology*, **43**, 213–24.

Orchard-Mills, E., Alais, D., & Van der Burg, E. (2013a). Amplitude-modulated auditory stimuli influence selection of visual spatial frequencies. *Journal of Vision*, 13, 6, 1–17.

Orchard-Mills, E, Alais, D., & Van der Burg, E. (2013b). Cross-modal associations between vision, touch and audition influence visual search through top-down attention, not bottom-up capture. *Attention, Perception & Psychophysics*, **75**, 1892–1905.

Orchard-Mills, E., Van der Burg, E., & Alais, D. (2016). Crossmodal correspondence between auditory pitch and visual elevation affects temporal ventriloquism. *Perception*, **45**, 409–24.

Orioli, G., Bremner, A. J., & Farroni, T. (2018). Multisensory perception of looming and receding objects in human newborns. *Current Biology*, **28**, R1283–R1295.

Oskarsson, P.-A., Eriksson, L., & Carlander, O. (2012). Enhanced perception and performance by multimodal threat cueing in simulated combat vehicle. *Human Factors*, **54**, 122–37.

Otten, L. J., Alain, C., & Picton, T. W. (2000). Effects of visual attentional load on auditory processing. *NeuroReport*, **11**, 875–80.

Otto, T. U., & Mamassian, P. (2012). Noise and correlations in parallel perceptual decision making. *Current Biology*, **22**, 1391–6.

Overvliet, K. O., Azañón, E., & Soto-Faraco, S. (2011). Somatosensory saccades reveal the timing of tactile spatial remapping. *Neuropsychologia*, **49**, 3046–52.

Oving, A. B., Veltmann, J. A., & Bronkhorst, A. W. (2004). Effectiveness of 3-D audio for warnings in the cockpit. *International Journal of Aviation Psychology*, **14**, 257–76.

Oyer, J., & Hardick, J. (1963). *Response of population to optimum warning signal*. Office of Civil Defence, Final Report No. SHSLR163. Contract No. OCK-OS-62–182, September.

Palmiero, M., Piccardi, L., Boccia, M., Baralla, F., Cordellieri, P., Sgalla, R., Guidoni, U., & Giannini, A. M. (2019). Neural correlates of simulated driving while performing a secondary task: A review. *Frontiers in Psychology*, **10**, 1045. http://doi.org/10.3389/fpsyg.2019.01045

Pápai, M. S. (2017). Behavioral and electrophysiological correlates of cross-modal enhancement for unaware visual events (Doctoral dissertation, Universitat Pompeu Fabra). https://www.tdx.cat/handle/10803/664283

Pápai, M. S., & Soto-Faraco, S. (2017). Sounds can boost the awareness of visual events through attention without cross-modal integration. *Scientific Reports*, **7**, 41684.

Parks, N. A., Hilimire, M. R., & Corballis, P. M. (2009). Visual perceptual load modulates an auditory microreflex. *Psychophysiology*, **46**, 498–501.

Pashler, H. (1992). Attentional limitations in doing two tasks at the same time. *Current Directions in Psychological Science*, **1**, 44–8.

Pashler, H. (1994). Dual-task interference in simple tasks: Data and theory. *Psychological Bulletin*, **116**, 220–44.

Pashler, H., Johnston, J. C., & Ruthruff, E. (2001). Attention and performance. *Annual Review of Psychology*, **52**, 629–51.

Patten, C. J. D., Kircher, A., Ostlund, J., & Nilsson, L. (2004). Using mobile telephones: Cognitive workload and attention resource allocation. *Accident Analysis & Prevention*, **36**, 341–50.

Peelen, M. V., & Kastner, S. (2014). Attention in the real world: Toward understanding its neural basis. *Trends in Cognitive Sciences*, **18**, 242–50.

Perrott, D. R., Cisneros, J., McKinley, R. L., & D'Angelo, W. (1996). Aurally aided visual search under virtual and free-field listening conditions. *Human Factors*, **38**, 702–15.

Perrott, D. R., Saberi, K., Brown, K., & Strybel, T. Z. (1990). Auditory psychomotor coordination and visual search performance. *Perception & Psychophysics*, **48**, 214–26.

Perrott, D. R., Sadralodabai, T., Saberi, K., & Strybel, T. Z. (1991). Aurally aided visual search in the central visual field: Effects of visual load and visual enhancement of the target. *Human Factors*, **33**, 389–400.

Pjetermeijer, S., Bazilinskyy, P., Bengler, K., & de Winter, J. (2017). Take-over again: Investigating multimodal and directional TORs to get the driver back into the loop. *Applied Ergonomics*, **62**, 204–15.

Poliakoff, E., Ashworth, S., Lowe, C., & Spence, C. (2006). Vision and touch in ageing: Crossmodal selective attention and visuotactile spatial interactions. *Neuropsychologia*, **44**, 507–17.

Poliakoff, E., Miles, E., Li, X., & Blanchette, I. (2007). The effect of visual threat on spatial attention to touch. *Cognition*, **102**, 405–14.

Pomper, U., Keil, J., Foxe, J. J., & Senkowski, D. (2015). Intersensory selective attention and temporal orienting operate in parallel and are instantiated in spatially distinct sensory and motor cortices. *Human Brain Mapping*, **36**, 3246–59.

Pöppel, E. (1973). Comments on 'Visual system's view of acoustic space'. *Nature*, **243**, 231.

Populin, L. C., & Yin, T. C. T. (1998). Sensitivity of auditory cells in the superior colliculus to eye position in the behaving cat. In A. R. Palmer, A. Rees, Q. Summerfield, & R. Meddis (Eds.), *Psychophysical and physiological advances in hearing* (pp. 441–8). London, UK: Whurr.

Populin, L. C., & Yin, T. C. T. (2002). Bimodal interactions in the superior colliculus of the behaving cat. *Journal of Neuroscience*, **22**, 2826–34.

Posner, M. I. (1978). *Chronometric explorations of mind*. Hillsdale, NJ: Erlbaum.

Posner, M. I. (1990). Hierarchical distributed networks in the neuropsychology of selective attention. In A. Caramazza (Ed.), *Cognitive neuropsychology and neurolinguistics: Advances in models of cognitive function and impairment* (pp. 187–210). Hillsdale, NJ: Erlbaum.

Posner, M. I., & Cohen, Y. (1984). Components of visual orienting. In H. Bouma & D. G. Bouwhuis (Eds.), *Attention and performance: Control of language processes* (Vol. 10, pp. 531–56). Hillsdale, NJ: Erlbaum.

Potter, M. C., Chun, M. M., Banks, B. S., & Muckenhoupt, M. (1998). Two attentional deficits in serial target search: The visual attentional blink and an amodal task-switch deficit. *Journal of Experimental Psychology: Learning, Memory, & Cognition*, **24**, 979–92.

Pouget, A., Deneve, S., & Duhamel, J.-R. (2002). A computational perspective on the neural basis of multisensory spatial representations. *Nature Reviews Neuroscience*, **3**, 741–7.

Pouget, A., Deneve, S., & Duhamel, J.-R. (2004). A computational neural theory of multisensory spatial representations. In C. Spence & J. Driver (Eds.), *Crossmodal space and crossmodal attention* (pp. 123–40). Oxford, UK: Oxford University Press.

Pratt, J., & Abrams, R. A. (1999). Inhibition of return in discrimination tasks. *Journal of Experimental Psychology: Human Perception and Performance*, **25**, 229–42.

Previc, F. H. (1998). The neuropsychology of 3-D space. *Psychological Bulletin*, **124**, 123–64.

Previc, F. H. (2000). Neuropsychological guidelines for aircraft control stations. *IEEE Engineering in Medicine and Biology Magazine*, **19**, 81–8.

Prime, D. J., McDonald, J. J., Green, J., & Ward, L. M. (2008). When cross-modal attention fails: A controversy resolved? *Canadian Journal of Experimental Psychology*, **62**, 192–7.

Prinzmetal, W., McCool, C., & Park, S. (2005a). Attention: Reaction time and accuracy reveal different mechanisms. *Journal of Experimental Psychology: General*, **134**, 73–92.

Prinzmetal, W., Park, S., & Garrett, R. (2005b). Involuntary attention and identification accuracy. *Perception & Psychophysics*, **67**, 1344–53.

Proctor, R. W., & Vu, K.-P. L. (2016). Principles for designing interfaces compatible with human information processing. *International Journal of Human Computer Interaction*, **32**, 2–22.

Ramachandran, V. S., Altschuler, E. L., & Hillyer, S. (1997). Mirror agnosia. *Proceedings of the Royal Society London B*, **264**, 645–7.

Raymond, J. E., Shapiro, K. L., & Arnell, K. M. (1992). Temporary suppression of visual processing in an RSVP task: An attentional blink? *Journal of Experimental Psychology: Human Perception and Performance*, **18**, 849–60.

Redelmeier, D. A., & Tibshirani, R. J. (1997). Association between cellular-telephone calls and motor vehicle collisions. *New England Journal of Medicine*, **336**, 453–8.

Reed, C. L., Grubb, J. D., & Steele, C. (2006). Hands up: Attentional prioritization of space near the hand. *Journal of Experimental Psychology: Human Perception & Performance*, **32**, 166–77.

Rees, G., Frith, C., & Lavie, N. (2001). Processing of irrelevant visual motion during performance of an auditory attention task. *Neuropsychologia*, **39**, 937–49.

Reisberg, D. (1978). Looking where you listen: Visual cues and auditory attention. *Acta Psychologica*, **42**, 331–41.

Ribot, T. (1898). *The psychology of attention*. Chicago, IL: Open Court Publishing Company.

Richard, C. M., Wright, R. D., Ee, C., Prime, S. L., Shimizu, Y., & Vavrik, J. (2002). Effect of a concurrent auditory task on visual search performance in a driving-related image-flicker task. *Human Factors*, **44**, 108–19.

Risko, E. F., & Kingstone, A. (2011). Eyes wide shut: Implied social presence, eye tracking and attention. *Attention, Perception, & Psychophysics*, **73**, 291–6.

Risko, E. F., Richardson, D. C., & Kingstone, A. (2016). Breaking the fourth wall of cognitive science: Real-world social attention and the dual function of gaze. *Current Directions in Psychological Science*, **25**, 70–4.

Röder, B., & Büchel, C. (2009). Multisensory interactions within and outside the focus of visual spatial attention (commentary on Fairhall & Macaluso). *European Journal of Neuroscience*, **29**, 1245–6.

Röder, B., Rösler, F., & Spence, C. (2004). Early vision impairs tactile perception in the blind. *Current Biology*, **14**, 121–4.

Romei, V., Gross, J., & Thut, G. (2012). Sounds reset rhythms of visual cortex and corresponding human visual perception. *Current Biology*, **22**, 807–13. http://doi.org/10.1016/j.cub.2012.03.025

Rorden, C., & Driver, J. (1999). Does auditory attention shift in the direction of an upcoming saccade? *Neuropsychologia*, **37**, 357–77.

Rozin, P. (2006). Domain denigration and process preference in academic psychology. *Perspectives in Psychological Science*, **1**, 365–76.

Rudmann, D. S., & Strybel, T. Z. (1999). Auditory spatial facilitation of visual search performance: Effect of cue precision and distractor density. *Human Factors*, **41**, 146–60.

Ruzzoli, M., & Soto-Faraco, S. (2017). Modality-switching in the Simon task: The clash of reference frames. *Journal of Experimental Psychology: General*, **146**, 1478–97.

Sambo, C. F., & Iannetti, G. D. (2013). Better safe than sorry? The safety margin surrounding the body is increased by anxiety. *Journal of Neuroscience*, **33**, 14225–30. http://doi.org/10.1523/JNEUROSCI.0706–13.2013

Sanabria, D., Soto-Faraco, S., & Spence, C. (2007). Spatial attention modulates audiovisual interactions in apparent motion. *Journal of Experimental Psychology: Human Perception and Performance*, **33**, 927–37.

Sandhu, R., & Dyson, B. J. (2016). Cross-modal perceptual load: The impact of modality and individual differences. *Experimental Brain Research*, **234**, 1279–91.

Santangelo, V., Belardinelli, M. O., & Spence, C. (2007). The suppression of reflexive visual and auditory orienting when attention is otherwise engaged. *Journal of Experimental Psychology: Human Perception & Performance*, **33**, 137–48.

Santangelo, V., Finoia, P., Raffone, A., Olivetti Belardinelli, M., & Spence, C. (2008a). Perceptual load affects exogenous spatial orienting while working memory load does not. *Experimental Brain Research*, **184**, 371–82.

Santangelo, V., Ho, C., & Spence, C. (2008b). Capturing spatial attention with multisensory cues. *Psychonomic Bulletin & Review*, **15**, 398–403.

Santangelo, V., Olivetti Belardinelli, M., Spence, C., & Macaluso, E. (2009). Multisensory interactions between voluntary and stimulus-driven spatial attention mechanisms across sensory modalities. *Journal of Cognitive Neuroscience*, **21**, 2384–97.

Santangelo, V., & Spence, C. (2007a). Multisensory cues capture spatial attention regardless of perceptual load. *Journal of Experimental Psychology: Human Perception & Performance*, **33**, 1311–21.

Santangelo, V., & Spence, C. (2007b). Assessing the automaticity of the exogenous orienting of tactile attention. *Perception*, **36**, 1497–505.

Santangelo, V., & Spence, C. (2007c). Assessing the effect of verbal working memory load on visuo-spatial exogenous orienting. *Neuroscience Letters*, **413**, 105–9.

Santangelo, V., & Spence, C. (2008a). Is the exogenous orienting of spatial attention truly automatic? Evidence from unimodal and multisensory studies. *Consciousness and Cognition*, **17**, 989–1015.

Santangelo, V., & Spence, C. (2008b). Crossmodal attentional capture in an unspeeded simultaneity judgement task. *Visual Cognition*, **16**, 155–65.

Sarter, N. B. (2000). The need for multisensory interfaces in support of effective attention allocation in highly dynamic event-driven domains: The case of cockpit automation. *International Journal of Aviation Psychology*, **10**, 231–45.

Sarter, N. B. (2002). Multimodal information presentation in support of human-automation communication and coordination. In E. Salas (Ed.), *Advances in human performance and cognitive engineering research* (pp. 13–36). New York, NY: JAI Press.

Sarter, N. B. (2006). Multimodal human-machine interfaces: Design guidance and research challenges. *International Journal of Industrial Ergonomics*, **36**, 439–45.

Sarter, N. B. (2007). Multiple-resource theory as a basis for multimodal interface design: Success stories, qualifications, and research needs. In

A. F. Kramer, D. A. Wiegmann, & A. Kirlik (Eds.), *Attention: From theory to practice* (pp. 187–95). Oxford, UK: Oxford University Press.

Scerra, V., & Brill, J. C. (2012). Effect of task modality on dual-task performance, response time, and ratings of operator workload. *Proceedings of the Human Factors and Ergonomics Society Annual Meeting*, **56**, 1456–60.

Scharf, B. (1998). Auditory attention: The psychoacoustical approach. In H. Pashler (Ed.), *Attention* (pp. 75–117). London, UK: Psychology Press.

Schicke, T., & Röder, B. (2006). Spatial remapping of touch: Confusion of perceived stimulus order across hand and foot. *Proceedings of the National Academy of Sciences of the United States of America*, **103**, 11808–13. http://doi.org/10.1073/pnas.0601486103

Schicke, T., Bauer, F., & Röder, B. (2009). Interactions of different body parts in peripersonal space: How vision of the foot influences tactile perception at the hand. *Experimental Brain Research*, **192**, 703–15.

Schmitt, M., Postma, A., & de Haan, E. (2000). Interactions between exogenous auditory and visual spatial attention. *Quarterly Journal of Experimental Psychology*, **53A**, 105–30.

Schmitt, M., Postma, A., & de Haan, E. (2001). Cross-modal exogenous attention and distance effects in vision and hearing. *European Journal of Cognitive Psychology*, **13**, 343–68.

Schneider, K. A., & Bavelier, D. (2003). Components of visual prior entry. *Cognitive Psychology*, **47**, 333–66.

Schreiber, T., & White, T. L. (2013). Detect, reject, focus: The role of satiation and odor relevance in cross-modal attention. *Chemosensory Perception*, **6**, 170–8.

Schroeder, C. E., & Lakatos, P. (2009). Low-frequency neural oscillations as instruments of sensory selection. *Trends in Neurosciences*, **32**, 9–18.

Schumacher, E. H., Seymour, T. L., Glass, J. M., Fencsik, D. E., Lauber, E. J., Kieras, D. E., & Meyer, D. E. (2001). Virtually perfect time sharing in dual-task performance: Uncorking the central cognitive bottleneck. *Psychological Science*, **12**, 101–8.

Seigneuric, A., Durand, K., Jiang, T., Baudouin, J.-Y., & Schaal, B. (2010). The nose tells it to the eyes: Crossmodal associations between olfaction and vision. *Perception*, **39**, 1541–54.

Senders, J. W., Kristofferson, A. B., Levison, W. H., Dietrich, C. W., & Ward, J. L. (1967). The attentional demand of automobile driving. *Highway Research Record*, **195**, 15–33.

Seo, H.-S., Roidl, E., Müller, F., & Negoias, S. (2010). Odors enhance visual attention to congruent objects. *Appetite*, **54**, 544–9.

Serences, J. T., Shomstein, S., Leber, A. B., Golav, X., Egeth, H. E., & Yantis, S. (2005). Coordination of voluntary and stimulus-driven attentional control in human cortex. *Psychological Science*, **16**, 114–22.

Serino, A., Annella, L., & Avenanti, A. (2009). Motor properties of peripersonal space in humans. *PLoS One*, **4**, e6582.

Shiffrin, R. M., & Grantham, D. W. (1974). Can attention be allocated to sensory modalities? *Perception & Psychophysics*, **15**, 460–74.

Shomstein, S., & Yantis, S. (2004). Control of attention shifts between vision and audition in human cortex. *Journal of Neuroscience*, **24**, 10702–6.

Shore, D. I., Barnes, M. E., & Spence, C. (2006). The temporal evolution of the crossmodal congruency effect. *Neuroscience Letters*, **392**, 96–100.

Shore, D. I., Spence, C., & Klein, R. M. (2001). Visual prior entry. *Psychological Science*, **12**, 205–12.

Shore, D. I., Spry, E., & Spence, C. (2002). Confusing the mind by crossing the hands. *Cognitive Brain Research*, **14**, 153–63.

Simon, J. R. (1990). The effects of an irrelevant directional cue on human information processing. In R. W. Proctor & T. G. Reeve (Eds.), *Stimulus-response compatibility* (pp. 31–86). Amsterdam, NL: Elsevier Science.

Simon, J. R., & Craft, J. L. (1970). Effects of an irrelevant auditory stimulus on visual choice reaction time. *Journal of Experimental Psychology*, **86**, 272–4.

Sinnett, S., Costa, A., & Soto-Faraco, S. (2006). Manipulating inattentional blindness within and across sensory modalities. *Quarterly Journal of Experimental Psychology*, **59**, 1425–42.

Sivak, M. (1996). The information that drivers use: Is it indeed 90% visual? *Perception*, **25**, 1081–9.

Soret, R., Hurter, C., & Peysakhovich, V. (2019). Attentional orienting in real and virtual 360-degree environments: Applications to aeronautics. Paper presented at *The 11th ACM Symposium Conference*, June. http://doi.org/10.1145/3314111.3322871

Soto-Faraco, S., Biau, E., Moris-Fernandez, L., Ikumi, N., Kvasova, D., Ruzzoli, M., & Torralba, M. (2019). Multisensory integration in the real world. *Cambridge elements of perception*. Cambridge, UK: Cambridge University Press.

Soto-Faraco, S., Morein-Zamir, S., & Kingstone, A. (2005). On audiovisual spatial synergy: The fragility of the phenomenon. *Perception & Psychophysics*, **67**, 444–57.

Soto-Faraco, S., Navarra, J., & Alsius, A. (2004). Assessing automaticity in audiovisual speech integration: Evidence from the speeded classification task. *Cognition*, **92**, B13–B23.

Soto-Faraco, S., & Spence, C. (2002). Modality-specific auditory and visual temporal processing deficits. *Quarterly Journal of Experimental Psychology (A)*, **55**, 23–40.

Soto-Faraco, S., Spence, C., Fairbank, K., Kingstone, A., Hillstrom, A. P., & Shapiro, K. (2002). A crossmodal attentional blink between vision and touch. *Psychonomic Bulletin & Review*, **9**, 731–8.

Spence, C. (2008). Searching for the bottleneck in the brain. *Current Biology*, **18**, R965–R968.

Spence, C. (2010a). Crossmodal attention. *Scholarpedia*, **5**, 6309. http://doi .org/10.4249/scholarpedia.6309

Spence, C. (2010b). Crossmodal spatial attention. *Annals of the New York Academy of Sciences (The Year in Cognitive Neuroscience)*, **1191**, 182–200.

Spence, C. (2011a). Crossmodal correspondences: A tutorial review. *Attention, Perception, & Psychophysics*, **73**, 971–95.

Spence, C. (2011b). Assessing the consequences of tool-use for the representation of peripersonal space in humans. In T. McCormack, C. Hoerl, & S. Butterfill (Eds.), *Tool use and causal cognition* (pp. 220–47). Oxford, UK: Oxford University Press.

Spence, C. (2012). Drive safely with neuroergonomics. *The Psychologist*, **25**, 664–7.

Spence, C. (2014). Orienting attention: A crossmodal perspective. In A. C. Nobre & S. Kastner (Eds.), *The Oxford handbook of attention* (pp. 446–71). Oxford, UK: Oxford University Press.

Spence, C. (2018). Multisensory perception. In J. Wixted (Ed.-in-Chief), J. Serences (Vol. Ed.), *The Stevens' handbook of experimental psychology and cognitive neuroscience* (4th ed., Vol. 2, pp. 1–56). Hoboken, NJ: John Wiley & Sons.

Spence, C. (2019a). On the relative nature of (pitch-based) crossmodal correspondences. *Multisensory Research*, **32**, 235–65.

Spence, C. (2019b). Attending to the chemical senses. *Multisensory Research*, **32**, 635–64.

Spence, C., & Deroy, O. (2013b). How automatic are crossmodal correspondences? *Consciousness and Cognition*, **22**, 245–60. http://doi.org/ 10.1016/j.concog.2012.12.006

Spence, C. [J.], & Driver, J. (1994). Covert spatial orienting in audition: Exogenous and endogenous mechanisms. *Journal of Experimental Psychology: Human Perception and Performance*, **20**, 555–74.

Spence, C., & Driver, J. (1996). Audiovisual links in endogenous covert spatial attention. *Journal of Experimental Psychology: Human Perception and Performance*, **22**, 1005–30.

Spence, C., & Driver, J. (1997a). Audiovisual links in exogenous covert spatial orienting. *Perception & Psychophysics*, **59**, 1–22.

Spence, C., & Driver, J. (1997b). Cross-modal links in attention between audition, vision, and touch: Implications for interface design. *International Journal of Cognitive Ergonomics*, **1**, 351–73.

Spence, C., & Driver, J. (1999). A new approach to the design of multimodal warning signals. In D. Harris (Ed.), *Engineering psychology and cognitive ergonomics, Vol. 4: Job design, product design and human-computer interaction* (pp. 455–61). Hampshire: Ashgate Publishing.

Spence, C., & Driver, J. (2000). Attracting attention to the illusory location of a sound: Reflexive crossmodal orienting and ventriloquism. *NeuroReport*, **11**, 2057–61.

Spence, C., & Driver, J. (Eds.). (2004). *Crossmodal space and crossmodal attention*. Oxford: Oxford University Press.

Spence, C., & Ho, C. (2008a). Crossmodal information processing in driving. In C. Castro (Ed.), *Human factors of visual performance in driving* (pp. 187–200). Boca Raton, FL: CRC Press.

Spence, C., & Ho, C. (2008b). Multisensory warning signals for event perception and safe driving. *Theoretical Issues in Ergonomics Science*, **9**, 523–54.

Spence, C., & Ho, C. (2015a). Crossmodal attention: From the laboratory to the real world (and back again). In J. M. Fawcett, E. F. Risko, & A. Kingstone (Eds.), *The handbook of attention* (pp. 119–38). Cambridge, MA: MIT Press.

Spence, C., & Ho, C. (2015b). Multisensory perception. In D. A. Boehm-Davis, F. T. Durso, & J. D. Lee (Eds.), *Handbook of human systems integration* (pp. 435–48). Washington, DC: American Psychological Association.

Spence, C., Kettenmann, B., Kobal, G., & McGlone, F. P. (2000). Selective attention to the chemosensory modality. *Perception & Psychophysics*, **62**, 1265–71.

Spence, C., Kettenmann, B., Kobal, G., & McGlone, F. P. (2001a). Attention to olfaction: A psychophysical investigation. *Experimental Brain Research*, **138**, 432–7.

Spence, C., Kettenmann, B., Kobal, G., & McGlone, F. P. (2001b). Shared attentional resources for processing vision and chemosensation. *Quarterly Journal of Experimental Psychology*, **54A**, 775–83.

Spence, C., Kingstone, A., Shore, D. I., & Gazzaniga, M. S. (2001). Representation of visuotactile space in the split brain. *Psychological Science*, **12**, 90–3.

Spence, C., Lee, J., & Van der Stoep, N. (2017). Responding to sounds from unseen locations: Crossmodal attentional orienting in response to sounds presented from the rear. *European Journal of Neuroscience*, **13733**, 1–14. http://doi.org/10.1111/ejn.13733

Spence, C., Lloyd, D., McGlone, F., Nicholls, M. E. R., & Driver, J. (2000). Inhibition of return is supramodal: A demonstration between all possible pairings of vision, touch and audition. *Experimental Brain Research*, **134**, 42–8.

Spence, C., McDonald, J., & Driver, J. (2004). Exogenous spatial cuing studies of human crossmodal attention and multisensory integration. In C. Spence & J. Driver (Eds.), *Crossmodal space and crossmodal attention* (pp. 277–320). Oxford, UK: Oxford University Press.

Spence, C., & Ngo, M. K. (2012). Does attention or multisensory integration explain the crossmodal facilitation of masked visual target identification? In B. E. Stein (Ed.), *The new handbook of multisensory processing* (pp. 345–58). Cambridge, MA: MIT Press.

Spence, C., Nicholls, M. E. R., & Driver, J. (2001a). The cost of expecting events in the wrong sensory modality. *Perception & Psychophysics*, **63**, 330–6.

Spence, C., Nicholls, M. E. R., Gillespie, N., & Driver, J. (1998). Cross-modal links in exogenous covert spatial orienting between touch, audition, and vision. *Perception & Psychophysics*, **60**, 544–57.

Spence, C., Parise, C., & Chen, Y.-C. (2011). The Colavita visual dominance effect. In M. M. Murray & M. Wallace (Eds.), *Frontiers in the neural bases of multisensory processes* (pp. 523–50). Boca Raton, FL: CRC Press.

Spence, C., Pavani, F., & Driver, J. (2000). Crossmodal links between vision and touch in covert endogenous spatial attention. *Journal of Experimental Psychology: Human Perception & Performance*, **26**, 1298–319.

Spence, C., Pavani, F., & Driver, J. (2004a). Spatial constraints on visual-tactile crossmodal distractor congruency effects. *Cognitive, Affective, & Behavioral Neuroscience*, **4**, 148–69.

Spence, C., Pavani, F., Maravita, A., & Holmes, N. (2004b). Multisensory contributions to the 3-D representation of visuotactile peripersonal space in humans: Evidence from the crossmodal congruency task. *Journal of Physiology (Paris)*, **98**, 171–89.

Spence, C., Pavani, F., Maravita, A., & Holmes, N. P. (2008). Multi-sensory interactions. In M. C. Lin & M. A. Otaduy (Eds.), *Haptic rendering: Foundations, algorithms, and applications* (pp. 21–52). Wellesley, MA: AK Peters.

Spence, C., Ranson, J., & Driver, J. (2000). Crossmodal selective attention: Ignoring auditory stimuli presented at the focus of visual attention. *Perception & Psychophysics*, **62**, 410–24.

Spence, C., & Read, L. (2003). Speech shadowing while driving: On the difficulty of splitting attention between eye and ear. *Psychological Science*, **14**, 251–6.

Spence, C., & Santangelo, V. (2009). Capturing spatial attention with multi-sensory cues: A review. *Hearing Research*, **258**, 134–42.

Spence, C., Shore, D. I., & Klein, R. M. (2001). Multimodal prior entry. *Journal of Experimental Psychology: General*, **130**, 799–832.

Spence, C., & Squire, S. B. (2003). Multisensory integration: Maintaining the perception of synchrony. *Current Biology*, **13**, R519–R521.

Stanney, K., Samman, S., Reeves, L., Hale, K., Buff, W., Bowers, C., Goldiez, B., Nicholson, D., & Lackey, S. (2004). A paradigm shift in inter-active computing: Deriving multimodal design principles from behavioral and neurological foundations. *International Journal of Human-Computer Interaction*, **17**, 229–57.

Stein, B. E., & Meredith, M. A. (1993). *The merging of the senses*. Cambridge, MA: MIT Press.

Stevenson, R. A., Krueger Fister, J., Barnett, Z. P., Nidiffer, A. R., & Wallace, M. T. (2012). Interactions between the spatial and temporal stimulus factors that influence multisensory integration in human performance. *Experimental Brain Research*, **219**, 121–37.

Stevenson, R. J., & Attuquayefilo, T. (2013). Human olfactory consciousness and cognition: Its unusual features may not result from unusual functions but from limited neocortical processing resources. *Frontiers in Psychology*, **4**, 819.

Störmer, V. S. (2019). Orienting spatial attention to sounds enhances visual perception. *Current Opinion in Psychological Science*, **29**, 193–8.

Störmer, V. S., Feng, W., Martinez, A., McDonald, J. J., & Hillyard, S. A. (2016) Salient, irrelevant sounds reflexively induce alpha rhythm desynchronization in parallel with slow potential shifts in visual cortex. *Journal of Cognitive Neuroscience*, **28**, 433–45.

Störmer, V. S., McDonald, J. J., & Hillyard, S. A. (2009). Cross-modal cueing of attention alters appearance and early cortical processing of visual stimuli. *Proceedings of the National Academy of Sciences of the USA*, **106**, 22456–61.

Strayer, D. L., Cooper, J. M., Goethe, R. M., McCarty, M. M., Getty, D. J., & Biondi, F. (2019). Assessing the visual and cognitive demands of in-vehicle information systems. *Cognitive Research: Principles and Implications*, 4, 5.

Strayer, D. L., & Drews, F. A. (2007). Multitasking in the automobile. In A. F. Kramer, D. A. Wiegmann, & A. Kirlik (Eds.), *Attention: From theory to practice* (pp. 121–33). Oxford, UK: Oxford University Press.

Strayer, D. L., Drews, F. A., & Johnston, W. A. (2003). Cell phone-induced failures of visual attention during simulated driving. *Journal of Experimental Psychology: Applied*, **9**, 23–32.

Strayer, D. L., & Johnston, W. A. (2001). Driven to distraction: Dual-task studies of simulated driving and conversing on a cellular telephone. *Psychological Science*, **12**, 462–6.

Streicher, M. C., & Estes, Z. (2016). Multisensory interaction in product choice: Grasping a product affects choice of other seen products. *Journal of Consumer Psychology*, **26**, 556–65.

Suetomi, T., & Kido, K. (1997). *Driver behavior under a collision warning system – A driving simulator study*. SAE Technical Publication, 970279, **1242**, 75–81.

Szczepanski, S. M., & Kastner, S. (2013). Shifting attentional priorities: Control of spatial attention through hemispheric competition. *Journal of Neuroscience*, **33**, 5411–21.

Taffou, M., & Viaud-Delmon, I. (2014). Cynophobic fear adaptively extends peri-personal space. *Frontiers in Psychiatry*, **5**, 122.

Talsma, D., Doty, T. J., Strowd, R., & Woldorff, M. G. (2006). Attentional capacity for processing concurrent stimuli is larger across modalities than within a modality. *Psychophysiology*, **43**, 541–9.

Talsma, D., Doty, T. J., & Woldorff, M. G. (2007). Selective attention and audiovisual integration: Is attending to both modalities a prerequisite for early integration? *Cerebral Cortex*, **17**, 691–701.

Talsma, D., Senkowski, D., Soto-Faraco, S., & Woldorff, M. G. (2010). The multifaceted interplay between attention and multisensory integration. *Trends in Cognitive Sciences*, **14**, 400–10.

Talsma, D., & Woldorff, M. G. (2005). Attention and multisensory integration: Multiple phases of effects on the evoked brain activity. *Journal of Cognitive Neuroscience*, **17**, 1098–114.

Tang, X. Y., Wu, J. L., & Shen, Y. (2016). The interactions of multisensory integration with endogenous and exogenous attention. *Neuroscience & Biobehavioral Reviews*, **61**, 208–24.

Taylor-Clarke, M., Kennett, S., & Haggard, P. (2002). Vision modulates somatosensory cortical processing. *Current Biology*, **12**, 233–6.

Tellinghuisen, D. J., & Nowak, E. J. (2003). The inability to ignore auditory distractors as a function of visual task perceptual load. *Perception & Psychophysics*, **65**, 817–28.

Teneggi, C., Canzoneri, E., di Pellegrino, G., & Serino, A. (2013). Social modulation of peripersonal space boundaries. *Current Biology*, **23**, 406–11.

Thomas, N., & Flew, A. (2016). The multisensory integration of auditory distractors and visuospatial attention. *Journal of Vision*, **16**, 147.

Tipper, S. P., Lloyd, D., Shorland, B., Dancer, C., Howard, L. A., & McGlone, F. (1998). Vision influences tactile perception without proprioceptive orienting. *Neuroreport*, **9**, 1741–4.

Tipper, S. P., Phillips, N., Dancer, C., Lloyd, D., Howard, L. A., & McGlone, F. (2001). Vision influences tactile perception at body sites that cannot be viewed directly. *Experimental Brain Research*, **139**, 160–7.

Titchener, E. B. (1908). *Lectures on the elementary psychology of feeling and attention*. New York, NY: Macmillan.

Treisman, A. M., & Davies, A. (1973). Divided attention to ear and eye. In S. Kornblum (Ed.) *Attention and performance* (Vol 4, pp. 101–17). New York, NY: Academic Press.

Tsal, Y., & Benoni, H. (2010). Diluting the burden of load: Perceptual load effects are simply dilution effects. *Journal of Experimental Psychology: Human Perception and Performance*, **36**, 1645–57.

Turatto, M., Benso, F., Galfano, G., Gamberini, L., & Umiltà, C. (2002). Non-spatial attentional shifts between audition and vision. *Journal of Experimental Psychology: Human Perception & Performance*, **28**, 628–39.

Turatto, M., Galfano, G., Bridgeman, B., & Umiltà, C. (2004). Space-independent modality-driven attentional capture in auditory, tactile and visual systems. *Experimental Brain Research*, **155**, 301–10.

Turatto, M., Mazza, V., & Umiltà, C. (2005). Crossmodal object-based attention: Auditory objects affect visual processing. *Cognition*, **96**, B55–B64.

Van Damme, S., Crombez, G., & Spence, C. (2009). Is the visual dominance effect modulated by the threat value of visual and auditory stimuli? *Experimental Brain Research*, **193**, 197–204.

Van Damme, S., Gallace, A., Spence, C., Crombez, G., & Moseley, G. L. (2009). Does the sight of physical threat induce a tactile processing bias? Modality-specific attentional facilitation induced by viewing threatening pictures. *Brain Research*, **1253**, 100–6.

Van der Burg, E., Olivers, C. N. L., Bronkhorst, A. W., Koelewijn, T., & Theeuwes, J. (2007). The absence of an auditory-visual attentional blink is not due to echoic memory. *Perception & Psychophysics*, **69**, 1230–41.

Van der Burg, E., Olivers, C. N. L., Bronkhorst, A. W., & Theeuwes, J. (2008a). Pip and pop: Non-spatial auditory signals improve spatial visual search. *Journal of Experimental Psychology: Human Perception and Performance*, **34**, 1053–65.

Van der Burg, E., Olivers, C. N. L., Bronkhorst, A. W., & Theeuwes, J. (2008b). Audiovisual events capture attention: Evidence from temporal order judgments. *Journal of Vision*, 8(2), 1–10.

van der Lubbe, R. H. J., & Postma, A. (2005). Interruption from auditory and visual onsets even when attention is in a focused state. *Experimental Brain Research*, **164**, 464–71.

Van der Stoep, N., Nijboer, T. C. W., Van der Stigchel, S., & Spence, C. (2015a). Multisensory interactions in the depth plane in front and rear space: A review. *Neuropsychologia*, **70**, 335–49.

Van der Stoep, N., Serino, A., Farnè, A., Di Luca, M., & Spence, C. (2016a). Depth: The forgotten dimension in multisensory research. *Multisensory Research*, **29**, 493–524.

Van der Stoep, N., Spence, C., Nijboer, T. C. W., & Van der Stigchel, S. (2015b). On the relative contributions of multisensory integration and crossmodal exogenous spatial attention to multisensory response enhancement. *Acta Psychologica*, **162**, 20–8.

Van der Stoep, N., Van der Stigchel, S., & Nijboer, T. C. (2015c). Exogenous spatial attention decreases audiovisual integration. *Attention, Perception, & Psychophysics*, **77**, 464–82.

Van der Stoep, N., Van der Stigchel, S., Nijboer, T. C. W., & Spence, C. (2017). Visually-induced inhibition of return affects the integration of auditory and visual information. *Perception*, **46**, 6–17.

Van der Stoep, N., Van der Stigchel, S., Nijboer, T. C. W., & Van der Smagt, M. J. (2016). Audiovisual integration in near and far space: Effects of changes in distance and stimulus effectiveness. *Experimental Brain Research*, **234**, 1175–88.

Van der Stoep, N., Visser-Meily, J. M., Kappelle, L. J., de Kort, P. L., Huisman, K. D., Eijsackers, A. L., et al. (2013). Exploring near and far regions of space: Distance-specific visuospatial neglect after stroke. *Journal of Clinical and Experimental Neuropsychology*, **35**, 799–811.

van der Wal, R. C., & Van Dillen, L. F. (2013). Leaving a flat taste in your mouth: Task load reduces taste perception. *Psychological Science* **24**, 1277–84.

van Elk, M., Forget, J., & Blanke, O. (2013). The effect of limb crossing and limb congruency on multisensory integration in peripersonal space for the upper and lower extremities. *Consciousness and Cognition*, **22**, 545–55.

Van Wassenhove, V., Grant, K. W., & Poeppel, D. (2005). Visual speech speeds up the neural processing of auditory speech. *Proceedings of the National Academy of Sciences of the USA*, **102**, 1181–6.

Vibell, J., Klinge, C., Zampini, M., Nobre, A. C., & Spence, C. (2017). Differences between endogenous attention to spatial locations and sensory modalities. *Experimental Brain Research*, **19**, 109–20.

Vibell, J., Klinge, C., Zampini, M., Spence, C., & Nobre, A. C. (2007). Temporal order is coded temporally in the brain: Early ERP latency shifts underlying prior entry in a crossmodal temporal order judgment task. *Journal of Cognitive Neuroscience*, **19**, 109–20.

Vroomen, J., Bertelson, P., & de Gelder, B. (2001a). The ventriloquist effect does not depend on the direction of automatic visual attention. *Perception & Psychophysics*, **63**, 651–9.

Vroomen, J., Bertelson, P., & de Gelder, B. (2001b). Directing spatial attention towards the illusory location of a ventriloquized sound. *Acta Psychologica*, **108**, 21–33.

Wahn, B., Keshava, A., Sinnett, S., Kingstone, A., & König, P. (2017). Audiovisual integration is affected by performing a task jointly. *Proceedings of the 39th Annual Conference of the Cognitive Science Society (Austin, TX)*, 1296–1301.

Wahn B., & König P. (2015a). Audition and vision share spatial attentional resources, yet attentional load does not disrupt audiovisual integration. *Frontiers in Psychology*, **6**, 1084. http://doi.org/10.3389/fpsyg.2015.01084

Wahn B., & König P. (2015b). Vision and haptics share spatial attentional resources and visuotactile integration is not affected by high attentional load. *Multisensory Research*, **28**, 371–92. http://doi.org/10.1163/22134808-00002482

Wahn, B., & König, P. (2016). Attentional resource allocation in visuotactile processing depends on the task, but optimal visuotactile integration does not depend on attentional resources. *Frontiers in Integrative Neuroscience*, **10**, 13.

Wahn, B., & König P. (2017). Is attentional resource allocation across sensory modalities task-dependent? *Advances in Cognitive Psychology*, **13**, 83–96. http://doi.org/10.5709/acp-0209-2

Wahn B., Murali, S., Sinnett, S., & König P. (2017). Auditory stimulus detection partially depends on visuospatial attentional resources. *i-Perception*, **8**, 1–17. http://doi.org/10.1177/2041669516688026

Wang, L., Yue, Z., & Chen, Q. (2012). Cross-modal nonspatial repetition inhibition. *Attention, Perception, & Psychophysics*, **74**, 867–78.

Ward, L. M. (1994). Supramodal and modality-specific mechanisms for stimulus-driven shifts of auditory and visual attention. *Canadian Journal of Experimental Psychology*, **48**, 242–59.

Ward, L. M., McDonald, J. A., & Golestani, N. (1998). Cross-modal control of attention shifts. In R. Wright (Ed.), *Visual attention* (pp. 232–68). New York, NY: Oxford University Press.

Ward, L. M., McDonald, J. J., & Lin, D. (2000). On asymmetries in cross-modal spatial attention orienting. *Perception & Psychophysics*, **62**, 1258–64.

Warm, J. S., Dember, W. N., & Parasuraman, R. (1991). Effects of olfactory stimulation on performance and stress in a visual sustained attention task. *Journal of the Society of Cosmetic Chemists*, **42**, 199–210.

Watt, R. J. (1991). *Understanding vision*. London, UK: Academic Press.

Weidler, B., & Abrams, R. A. (2014). Enhanced cognitive control near the hands. *Psychonomic Bulletin & Review*, **21**, 462–9.

Welford, A. T. (1952). The 'psychological refractory period' and the timing of high-speed performance – A review and a theory. *British Journal of Psychology*, **43**, 2–19.

Wickens, C. D. (1984). Processing resources in attention. In R. Parasuraman & D. R. Davies (Eds.), *Varieties of attention* (pp. 63–102). San Diego, CA: Academic Press.

Wickens, C. D. (1992). *Engineering psychology and human performance* (2nd ed.). New York, NY: HarperCollins.

Wickens, C. D. (2002). Multiple resources and performance prediction. *Theoretical Issues in Ergonomics Science*, **3**, 159–77.

Witt, J. K., Proffitt, D. R., & Epstein, W. (2005). Tool use affects perceived distance, but only when you intend to use it. *Journal of Experimental Psychology: Human Perception and Performance*, **31**, 880–8.

Wogalter, M. S., Kalsher, M. J., & Racicot, B. M. (1993). Behavioral compliance with warnings: Effects of voice, context, and location. *Safety Science*, **16**, 637–54.

Wolfe, J. M., Horowitz, T. S., & Kenner, N. M. (2005). Rare items often missed in visual searches. *Nature*, **435**, 439–40. http://doi.org/10.1038/435439a

Woodrow, H. (1914). The measurement of attention. *The Psychological Monographs*, **17**, i–158. http://doi.org/10.1037/h0093087

Wozny, D. R., Beierholm, U. R., & Shams, L. (2008). Human trimodal perception follows optimal statistical inference. *Journal of Vision*, **8**, 24, 1–11.

Wu, C.-C., Wick, F. A., & Pomplun, M. (2014). Guidance of visual attention by semantic information in real-world scenes. *Frontiers in Psychology*, **5**, 54. http://doi.org/10.3389/fpsyg.2014.00054

Wu, J., Li, Q., Bai, O., & Touge, T. (2009). Multisensory interactions elicited by audiovisual stimuli presented peripherally in a visual attention task: A behavioral and event-related potential study in humans. *Journal of Clinical Neurophysiology*, **26**, 407–13.

Yamamoto, S., & Kitazawa, S. (2001). Reversal of subjective temporal order due to arm crossing. *Nature Neuroscience*, **4**, 759–65.

Yue, Z., Bischof, G.-N., Zhou, X., Spence, C., & Röder, B. (2009). Spatial attention affects the processing of tactile and visual stimuli presented at the tip of a tool: An event-related potential study. *Experimental Brain Research*, **193**, 119–28.

Yue, Z., Jiang, Y., Li, Y., Wang, P., & Chen, Q. (2015). Enhanced visual dominance in far space. *Experimental Brain Research*, **233**, 2833–43.

Zampini, M., Guest, S., Shore, D. I., & Spence, C. (2005). Audiovisual simultaneity judgments. *Perception & Psychophysics*, **67**, 531–44.

Zampini, M., Torresan, D., Spence, C., & Murray, M. M. (2007). Audiotactile multisensory interactions in front and rear space. *Neuropsychologia*, **45**, 1869–77.

Zangenehpour, S., & Zatorre, R. J. (2010). Cross-modal recruitment of primary visual cortex following brief exposure to bimodal audiovisual stimuli. *Neuropsychologia*, **48**, 591–600.

Zimmer, U., & Macaluso, E. (2007). Processing of multisensory spatial congruence can be dissociated from working memory and visuo-spatial attention. *European Journal of Neuroscience*, **26**, 1681–91.

Zmigrod, S., Spapé, M., & Hommel, B. (2009). Intermodal event files: Integrating features across vision, audition, taction, and action. *Psychological Research*, **73**, 674–84.

Zou, H., Müller, H. J., & Shi, Z. (2012). Non-spatial sounds regulate eye movements and enhance visual search. *Journal of Vision*, **12**, 1–18.

Cambridge Elements ≡

Perception

James T. Enns
The University of British Columbia

Editor James T. Enns is Professor at the University of British Columbia, where he researches the interaction of perception, attention, emotion, and social factors. He has previously been Editor of the *Journal of Experimental Psychology: Human Perception and Performance* and an Associate Editor at *Psychological Science, Consciousness and Cognition, Attention Perception & Psychophysics,* and *Visual Cognition.*

Editorial Board

About the Series

The modern study of human perception includes event perception, bidirectional influences between perception and action, music, language, the integration of the senses, human action observation, and the important roles of emotion, motivation, and social factors. Each Element in the series combines authoritative literature reviews of foundational topics with forward-looking presentations of the recent developments on a given topic.

Cambridge Elements ≡

Perception

Elements in the Series

A full series listing is available at: www.cambridge.org/EPER

Printed in the United States
By Bookmasters